Learning from the Land
Wisconsin Land Use

2nd Edition

Bobbie Malone, PhD

Wisconsin Historical Society Press

Published by the Wisconsin Historical Society Press
Publishers since 1855

© 1998, 2011 by the State Historical Society of Wisconsin

For permission to reuse material from *Learning from the Land: Wisconsin Land Use, 2nd Edition,* 978-0-087020-464-7, please access www.copyright.com or contact the Copyright Clearance Center, Inc. (CCC), 222 Rosewood Drive, Danvers, MA 01923, 978-750-8400. CCC is a not-for-profit organization that provides licenses and registration for a variety of users.

wisconsinhistory.org

Photographs identified with WHi or WHS are from the Society's collections; address requests to reproduce these photos to the Visual Materials Archivist at the Wisconsin Historical Society, 816 State Street, Madison, WI 53706.

Printed in the United States of America
Designed by Jill Bremigan
Badger illustrations by Jill Bremigen

15 14 13 12 11   1 2 3 4 5

Library of Congress Cataloging-in-Publication Data
Malone, Bobbie, 1944–

Learning from the land : Wisconsin land use / Bobbie Malone.—2nd ed.

p. cm.— (New badger history series)

Includes index.

ISBN 978-0-87020-464-7 (pbk. : alk. paper) 1. Land use—Wisconsin—History—Juvenile literature. 2. Land use, Rural—Wisconsin—History—Juvenile literature. 3. Land settlement—Wisconsin—History—Juvenile literature. 4. Human settlements—Wisconsin—History—Juvenile literature. 5. Agricultural industries—Wisconsin—Juvenile literature. 6. Wisconsin—History—Juvenile literature. I. Wisconsin Historical Society. II. Title.

HD211.W6M35 2011

333.73'1309775–dc22

2010051100

∞ The paper used in this publication meets the minimum requirements of the American National Standard for Information Sciences—Permanence of Paper for Printed Library Materials, ANSI Z39.48-1992.

**Other Titles in the
New Badger History Series**
(Includes classroom texts
and teacher guides)

*Digging and Discovery:
Wisconsin Archaeology*

Native People of Wisconsin

They Came to Wisconsin

*Voices & Votes: How Democracy
Works in Wisconsin*

*Working with Water:
Wisconsin Waterways*

Learning from the Land
Wisconsin Land Use

Contents

Introduction: Changes and Choices viii

Chapter One: The Land Where We Stand 2
Think About It. 3
The Land Has Its Own Story 4
Of Ice and Land. 5
Of Rock and Regions 7
Of Climate, Soils, and Vegetation 10

Chapter Two: The First Land Shapers 14
Think About It. 15
Living from the Land's Resources 16
Finding Special Places 17
The Meaning of Mounds 20
The First Farmers 22

**Chapter Three: The Fur Trade Brings
New Ways of Living** 26
Think About It. 27
Wisconsin Indian Traditions. 28
Living with the Land 29
The Fur Trade 32
New Attitudes. 35

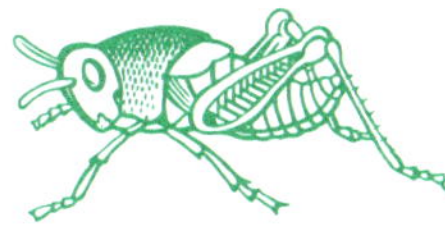

Chapter Four: Treaty Making and Land Taking .. 38

Think About It. 39
Treaties and Trouble 40
Before Black Hawk 44
On the Lookout for Lead 45
The Black Hawk War 49

Chapter Five: Surveying, Selling, and Settling the Land 56

Think About It. 57
Laws About Land 58
Surveying the Land 59
Selling the Land 61
Settling the Land 63

Chapter Six: Timber! 70

Think About It. 71
Native People and Wisconsin Forests. 72
Our Forests Build a New State and Nation 72
The Lumber Industry: Risk, Growth, and New Technology 78
The Forests: Logged and Burned. 80
Champions of the Forest 85
Rebuilding and Sustainably Caring for Our Forests. . . . 88

Chapter Seven: From Wheat to Milk and More . . 92

Think About It. 93
Looking Back. 94
Wisconsin as a Breadbasket 95
Becoming the Dairy State 98
Changes in Dairyland 103
   Many Farms, Many Crops, Many Different People 105
   Selling What You Grow 106
   Eating and Buying Locally 111
   Growing Soil, Growing Vegetables, Growing Healthy . . 114

Chapter Eight: Living with the Land 120

Think About It. 121
Looking Back. 122
A Lover of the Land 125
Designing for Tomorrow. 128
Protecting Our Planet 131

Glossary 135

Index 154

Acknowledgments. 160

Introduction

Changes and Choices

Have you ever wondered what's special about the place we call Wisconsin? Just what is so special about the way people lived here in the past? How is it different from or similar to the way we live

A Cross Plains farm tucked next to a hillside

in our state today? How are those ways of living and learning from the land different from the way people have lived in other places? In *Learning from the Land,* you'll find the answers to these questions and others.

Wisconsin is large enough to have more than one kind of **landscape** . You'll learn how Wisconsin's landscape and **environment** (en **vi** ruhn muhnt) changed many times over millions of years before people could begin to live here. Then, you'll learn about the changes that people made to the land they found. Those human-made changes are known as **land use** . *Learning from the Land* tells the story of how land use in different parts of Wisconsin has changed from the time the first people settled here thousands of years ago to the way we use land today.

The Ice Age trail stretches all the way across Wisconsin! Many people use the trail for biking and walking.

People often have very different ideas about how to use the land we share. Should the community put a new tennis court or a soccer field in the park? Tennis players want the court. Soccer teams want the field. Someone might want to build shopping centers or high-rise apartments in the same area where others want to create **nature preserves** (pri **zurvz**), farms, or homes with yards. Sometimes these ideas about how to use land cause **conflict** (**kon** flikt). Not everyone will be pleased with the decision.

---

landscape: A large area of land that you can view from one place   **environment:** The natural world of land, sea, soil, and air in which people, animals, and plants live   **land use:** The way people have changed the land where they live by building on it, plowing it, making roads across it, and creating settlements or cities   **nature preserves:** Areas where wild animals, fish, or trees and plants are protected   **conflict:** Disagreement

viii

For example, people often object to the noise and traffic that a new shopping center brings to their neighborhood. Others are glad that their favorite stores are within walking distance of their homes. Those who would rather see a shopping center would not be thrilled with those who would like to create a nature preserve. But people who want to create a nature preserve may also want people to be able to enjoy biking, walking, and hiking.

Dairy farmers don't want the highway that borders their farms to be widened and replace the part of the land where their cattle grazes in the summer months. The wider highway reduces land that the farmers need for their herds. But truck drivers who regularly use the highway want to see it widened so that it is easier and safer to drive.

As these examples show, people sometimes have the ability to *choose* the kinds of land use they want to see. Some choices have been good for the land. Others have not. Some changes please most people. Others don't. Both natural changes and those that people continue to make are still changing Wisconsin's landscape.

All of these people see and value the land in different ways. We can discover a great deal of the history of our state in the choices that people have made about using the land, and in the changes those choices created. Sometimes people didn't realize that their choices would lead to changes in the land itself.

As you read *Learning from the Land* you'll have a chance to think about these choices. As you learn more about the way people's choices in land use have **affected** (uh **fek** ted) our environment, you'll learn how to make good choices yourself.

affected: Influenced or changed

Copper Falls State Park on the Bad River in Mellen, Wisconsin

This house was destroyed to make room for the Kohl Center in Madison.

Chapter 1

The Land Where We Stand

◆ ◆ ◆

Thinking about land use allows you to create images in your mind. You can picture a **rural** setting where there are farm fields, highways, and roadside shops to stop for gas or food. Or you can picture a town with its houses, roads, shopping areas, playgrounds, schools, and parks. You may have never thought about how Wisconsin looked before people began living in your area. Yet there was a time when nothing human-made could be seen in the landscape of Wisconsin. And even those many, many years ago, the land was still changed by natural rather than human forces.

Abbotsford Elementary School

Before humans came to Wisconsin, most of what was seen was the **natural environment** . When humans came, we built on the land and created roads, making what is called the **built environment** . This chapter explores what happened to the land we live on before a single human set foot on it.

rural: Having to do with farms or the country   natural environment: The original features that make up a landscape, such as trees, rivers, and animals   built environment: The human-made features that make up a landscape, such as houses, buildings, and roads

2

Think About It

How was land in Wisconsin shaped by natural forces? What different kinds of land are there in Wisconsin? What kinds of soil? In what ways did the land and soil of different **regions** (**ree** juns) within Wisconsin affect people's choices about where to live and how to live?

Wisconsin's first state park, Interstate State Park, is located on the St. Croix River.

regions: Areas defined by common features, such as a similar landscape

3

The Land Has Its Own Story

Geologists (jee **ol** uh jists) are scientists who study the layers of rock that form the earth. Geologists explain how the land changed millions and billions of years before people lived here. They have found that some of Wisconsin's **bedrock** is among the oldest in the world.

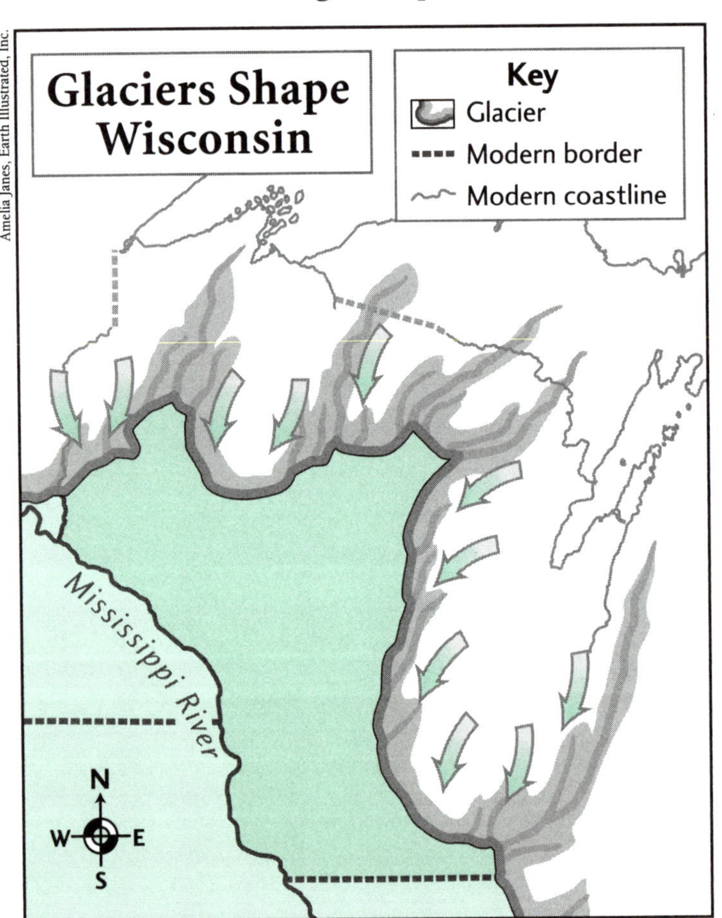

Other Wisconsin rock developed more recently. Earthquakes and volcanoes shaped the landscape a billion years ago.

Then, about 400 million years ago, a warm, shallow sea covered the area that became Wisconsin.

Finally, the first **glaciers** (**glay** shurz), or sheets of ice, seeped down from the north to cover most of Wisconsin about a million years ago. The last glaciers were still melting when Wisconsin's first people lived here.

geologists: Scientists who study the layers of rock that form the earth and looser rock   **glaciers:** Sheets of ice that cover large areas of land   **bedrock:** The solid rock that lies under the soil

Of Ice and Land

The movement of glaciers was the last major **geological** (jee uh **loj** uh kuhl) change that occurred in our region. One way of looking at land in Wisconsin, in fact, is to divide it into 2 areas.

The largest area in the north and east was once covered by glaciers. That's why we say it is **glaciated** (**glay** shee ay tuhd). At one time glaciers covered about three-fourths of Wisconsin! The ice sheets pushed, dragged, and carried rocks and soils along with them as they moved.

As the climate warmed, the ice sheets melted very slowly. As the glaciers shrank, they left behind **glacial drift**, the soil and rock that had been frozen in the ice.

Shrinking glaciers reshaped the surface of the land and **transformed** the contents of its soils. The heavy layers of ice smoothed out the land's rough edges in some places. In other places, the melting ice left the land

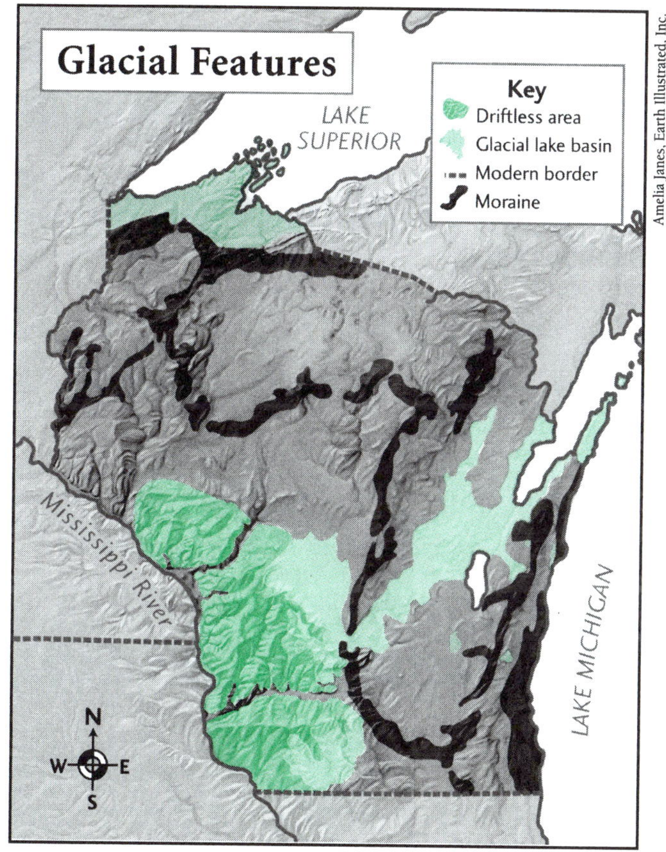

---

geological: Having to do with the study of the layers of rock that form the earth   **glaciated:** Once covered by large sheets of ice   **glacial drift:** The soil and rock that has been moved by ice   **transformed:** Changed in major ways

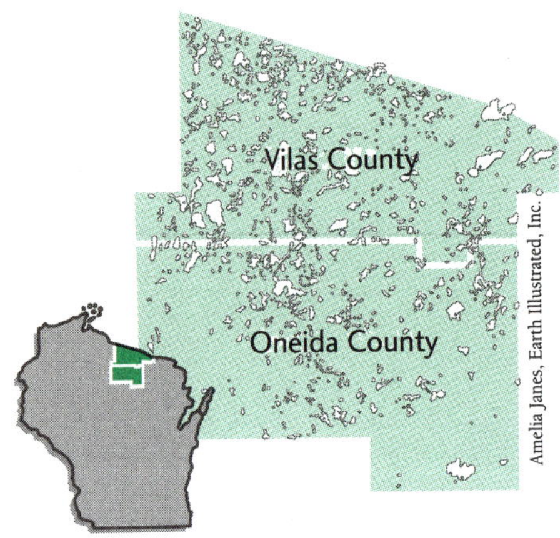
Many lakes created by glaciers fill Vilas and Oneida counties.

lumpy with many lakes and **wetlands**. In fact, Vilas and Oneida counties in northeast Wisconsin contain nearly 2,000 lakes!

But glaciers never covered the southwest quarter of Wisconsin. That's why we say it is **unglaciated**. Because southwest Wisconsin has no glacial drift, people often call this part of the state the Driftless Area.

No glaciers smoothed the **topography** (tuh **pog** ruh fee), or physical shape, of the Driftless Area. So the Driftless Area is very different from the rest of the state.

Steep hills and deep river valleys mark the Wisconsin Dells in the Driftless area.

When you visit the Driftless Area, you can see strange rock formations, cliffs, and steep-sided valleys that are not found in the rest of the state. Its rivers cut deep **gorges** (**gor** juhz) or canyons between the rocks.

The Mississippi River flows along more than half of Wisconsin's western border. The Mississippi River valley

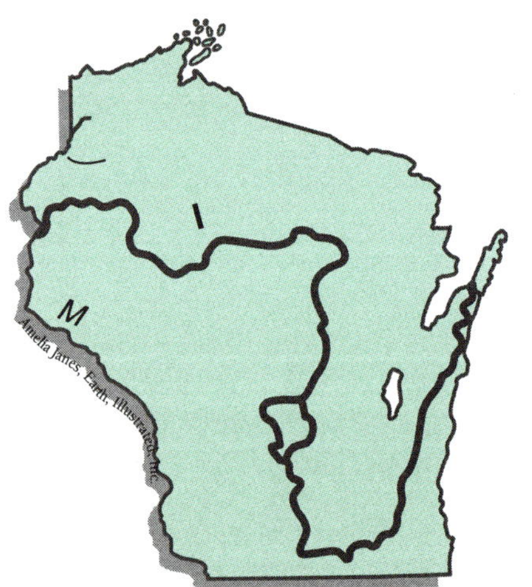
Compare this map of the Ice Age Trail to the map on page 4. What do you notice about the location of the trail?

wetlands: Areas covered with water for all or part of the year **unglaciated:** Not covered in the past by large sheets of ice
topography: The physical features of the land that shape its landscape, such as mountains, valleys, plains, and rivers
gorges: Large spaces between rocks

forms the largest of these gorges. Visiting the Driftless Area gives us a good idea of how most of the rest of the state looked before the Ice Age, when glaciers spread south from Canada and covered much of Wisconsin.

Of Rock and Regions

Geographers (jee **og** ruh furz) are scientists who study the earth's **physical features**. Geographers also study the people, resources, and weather patterns of different areas.

Geographers usually divide Wisconsin into 5 major regions. These regions are defined by different kinds of bedrock. Although most of this rock base cannot be seen, it is very important. Bedrock shapes the way the rivers run and how the land drains. It also affects which natural plants and crops can survive and do well in a particular location.

Look at the map of Wisconsin's 5 physical regions. You can see that a shallow scoop on the northernmost portion of the state forms the **Lake Superior Lowland**. Immediately to the south of this region comes the **Northern Highland**, the largest of Wisconsin's regions.

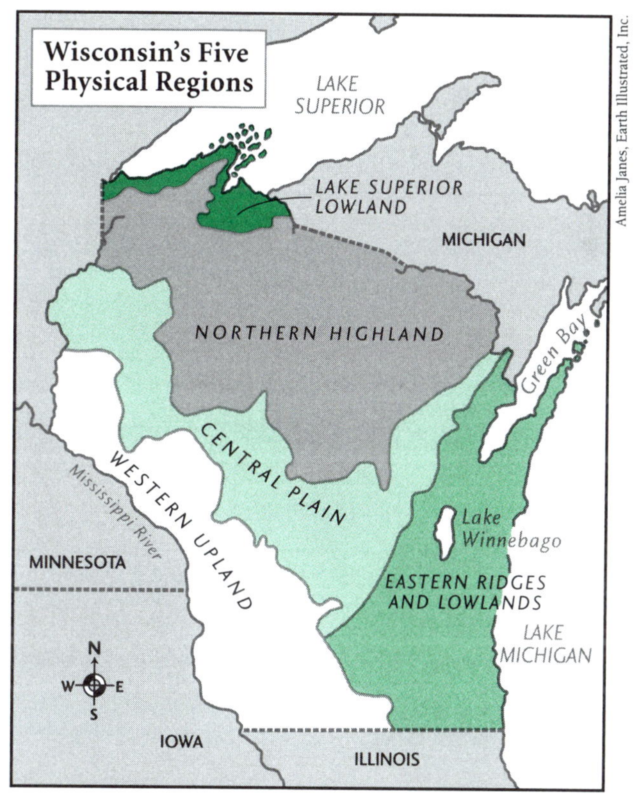

geographers: Scientists who study the earth, including its people, resources, climate, and physical features
physical features: The appearance of the land, including its mountains, rivers, and plants

The **Central Plain** makes a rough V shape in the middle of the state. It separates the Northern Highlands from the **Eastern Ridges and Lowlands** that border Lake Michigan and from the **Western Upland** that runs along the Mississippi River on the west. The Driftless Area forms a large part of the Western Upland.

Long before the Ice Age, a great earthquake shook the Lake Superior Lowland. One section of land caved in and made a huge **trench**. This trench went through many physical changes.

At times, the land that formed the trench rose and fell again. The land and water around this trench also changed. More than once, this trench was filled with water or covered with ice. At other times, the area was completely dry. Today the Lake Superior Lowland slopes toward Lake Superior.

Yet the Lake Superior Lowland is hilly because long rivers cut their way through it. This region has **fertile** (**fur** tuhl) soil. The shore of Lake Superior protects the Lowland from the extremes of the cold northern winter. This protection helps give the Lake Superior Lowland a surprisingly long growing season.

Once, a high mountain range formed the gently rolling landscape known as the Northern Highland. The region is higher in the middle than along the edges. That's why rivers in the Northern Highland flow down in many different directions. Its rocks contain iron and copper ore, and its soil is rich. In the Northern Highland, forests are more common than farms.

The V-shaped Central Plain contains several different landscapes. The center and western areas are very flat. In the east, glaciers created stony hills and low spots called **kettles**. Often these kettles contain wetlands.

   trench: A long, deep, narrow hole   **fertile:** Good for growing crops   **kettles:** Scooped-out areas that were filled with large blocks of ice

The soil is sandy in the Central Plain. The poor soil limits the kind of plants that grow in this region. Many of Wisconsin's biggest rivers flow through this region, including the Wisconsin River and the Chippewa (**chip** uh wuh) and Fox rivers.

The landscape of the Eastern Ridges and Lowlands shows the powerful effects of glacial movement. This region includes Lake Winnebago (win uh **bay** goh), Horicon Marsh, and the Kettle **Moraine** (muh **rain**). Glaciers moved soils and rocks that made this soil the most fertile in the state.

The Eastern Ridges and Lowlands have a mild climate, a long growing season, and plenty of gently flowing rivers. Would these be good reasons to settle there? You betcha! Today, more people live in this region than in any other in the state. It's also home to Wisconsin's 2 largest cities: Milwaukee and Madison.

You can easily see the clear outlines of this long, low hill known as a moraine.

We don't often refer to big pots as "kettles" any more. But this lumpy-looking land with its numerous low spots reminded people of deep pots, and that's why these places are also called kettles.

One of many kettle ponds in the Kettle Moraine area in the Eastern Ridges and Lowlands

---

moraine: Soil and rocks left by glaciers that form ridges and low hills

The Western Upland contains most of the Driftless Area—the area of Wisconsin that was never touched by glaciers. The valleys are fertile and the ridges high, like at Devil's Lake or at Wyalusing (wI uh **loo** sing) State Park on the Mississippi. The rock overhangs are deep enough to provide natural shelters and many small caves.

The Western Upland also contains large **deposits** (di **poz** its) of lead and zinc. These **minerals** were important to people who later settled there and mined them.

Of Climate, Soils, and Vegetation

It isn't only people who decide what to do with land. Soil and climate also affect the choices people make. For instance, corn, Wisconsin's biggest crop, grows very well in the fertile Driftless region, but not so well in the sandy Central Plain. The soil map on the next page shows where various types of soil are located in the state.

This rock formation is known as Devil's Doorway. Beyond the rocks you can see the hill-like ridges that surround Devil's Lake near Baraboo.

WHi Image ID 63256

deposits: Natural layers of rock, sand, or minerals found in the ground   **minerals:** Solid substances like gold or copper, usually dug from the earth

SOILS OF WISCONSIN

The basic soil types are clay, sand, and silt. Some are good for growing plants, while others are not.

CLAY contains tiny bits of rock and minerals. When clay collects water, it becomes sticky. The clay in the soil helps it to stick together.

SAND particles hold very little water. When it rains, the water flows right through the sand. That's why plants have such a hard time growing in sandy soil.

SILT is between sand and clay. It absorbs water, but doesn't become sticky.

LOAM combines silt, clay, and sand. Plants grow well in loamy soil.

PEAT contains dead and decaying plant life. Sometimes it is found many feet deep. By itself, peat isn't good for growing plants. It does not contain all of the materials necessary for plant growth.

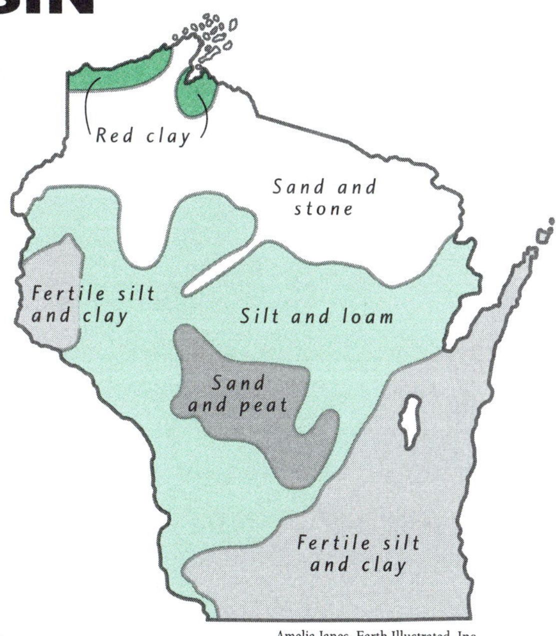

Amelia Janes, Earth Illustrated, Inc.

Wisconsin's climate and soil are different from north to south and from east to west. That means that the plants grown in these places are not the same. Southern Wisconsin has the state's longest growing season and generally richer soils. The long growing season and excellent soil support a great variety of plants and trees. The large stretches of Wisconsin prairie and **oak openings** in the south are very different from the pine forests in the north. Different kinds of bedrock, soil, and climate meant that people from one area lived differently from those in another.

Open prairie in southern Wisconsin with very few trees

Evergreens and other trees on Washington Island

Once the glaciers melted and people began living here, their choices changed the land—for better and for worse. How did their choices reshape the landscape, and how did these choices lead to conflicts about how people should use the land? That's the story you'll find in the rest of the book.

     oak openings: Prairies where oaks have been the only trees to survive past fires because of their thick bark

Learning about the history of land use will help us understand how these choices, changes, and conflicts occurred. We can also see that making better choices will help keep Wisconsin a good place to live. Some people believe that the name *Wisconsin* comes from an Indian name that means "a good place to live," although no one is sure. Wherever our state's name comes from, we *are* sure that we need to remember that *where* we live affects *how* we live. And the choices that people make about land use can help keep making our state "a good place to live."

Chapter 2

The First Land Shapers

◆ ◆ ◆

People have shaped the land around you—whether you are living in a crowded city, in a small town, or on a farm where corn is growing as far as you can see. People have plowed fields and planted crops, cut down trees and replanted forests, and mined for minerals. They have built roads, parking lots, playgrounds, shopping centers, office buildings, and houses. We can watch highways being built or repaired and think about the ways that people constantly shape and reshape the landscape in order to meet their needs and the needs of their community.

Many different groups of Indian people shared this land for thousands of years before the first non-Indian settlers entered Wisconsin, and these early Indians were also shapers of the land where they lived.

Construction workers repair Interstate 90.

Think About It

Who were the earliest people living here? How did they use and change the land? What are the effects of those changes that we can still see today?

Living from the Land's Resources

Indians began living here just as soon as the climate warmed enough to melt the last glaciers. **Archaeologists** (ahr kee **ol** uh jists) are scientists who learn how people lived by studying the things they have left behind. Archaeologists gave the name Paleo-Indians (**pay** lee oh) to these earliest people in Wisconsin.

Paleo-Indians began living here about 12,000 years ago. The last glacier was still melting at the time. Archaeologists have found only a few clues that tell us how Paleo-Indians lived so long ago. Stone spear points show that Paleo-Indian people made tools. Cut marks on animal bones show that people butchered these animals. Only stone or bone could survive that many years!

Archaeologists know that Paleo-Indians lived in rock shelters. They probably built homes of other materials, too. But these materials did not survive to tell that part of the Paleo-Indian story. For the same reason, we do not have evidence of the way Paleo-Indians dressed. But they would have had to wear animal skins and furs to survive in the much cooler climate thousands of years ago.

Living in Wisconsin was more difficult during the time Paleo-Indians were around. Few plants could survive in the cold climate. The small number of Paleo-Indians in the area lived mainly by hunting. And they had to travel great distances to find food. Some animals they hunted were huge **mammals**, such as **mastodons** (**mast** uh dons) and mammoths. These giant beasts are now **extinct**.

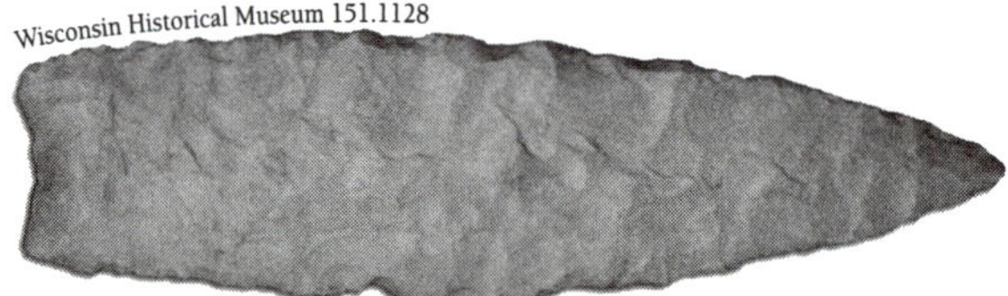

This Paleo spearhead was found by archaeologists in Wisconsin. What might its owners have used it for?

16

archaeologists: Scientists who learn how we lived in the past by studying the things people left in the places where they once lived   **mammals:** Warm-blooded animals with a backbone   **mastodons:** Large, hairy mammals, related to the elephant, that died out thousands of years ago   **extinct:** No longer exist

The climate gradually warmed up. The **era** of the giant mammals ended. Warmer weather made it easier for more types of plants to grow. These plants and trees grew into forests that attracted more animals, including fish and birds. Oak trees replaced pine trees in the southern part of the state, and deer and smaller animals grew in number. These **natural resources** could also support more people.

Archaeologists named the people who lived in this new environment Archaic (ahr **kay** ik) Indians. Archaeologists don't know if the Archaic Indians were directly **related** to the Paleo-Indians. But Archaic Indians could have moved into Wisconsin as the climate and resources improved. The Archaic people found new ways to live in the warmer environment.

A mastadon

Finding Special Places

The Archaic Indians lived in Wisconsin for about 6,000 years. They hunted smaller animals like deer, beaver, and birds. They enjoyed fishing in Wisconsin's lakes and rivers. They also gathered nuts and berries. Some Archaic Indian groups became Wisconsin's first miners. They made tools, jewelry, and weapons from copper found in the Northern Highlands. They also traded copper and other objects with tribes throughout the Great Lakes region.

era: A period of time in history   **natural resources:** Raw materials found in nature that may be used by people, like plants, water, animals, and minerals   **related:** Part of the same family

17

An Archaic Indian mines for copper.

Like the Paleo-Indians, the Archaic Indians most likely traveled in small groups to find food. But they did not have to travel so far because they could find more plant and animal resources locally. Archaic Indians could spend more time in a specific area. They also planned special times to **reunite** (ree yoo **nit**) with other small groups of community or family members.

Archaic people also understood the rhythm of the seasons. They knew when and where to find the resources they needed throughout the year. They used this knowledge to plan their yearly travel. That way, they could camp at places when the food supply was at its **peak** . Archaic people planned ahead for difficult times like late winter. That's when stored food supplies became low and fewer animals were available to hunt.

What Archaic people hunted, gathered, and stored depended on *where* they were living during different seasons of the year. The resources that Indians who traveled and camped in southwestern Wisconsin hunted and gathered were different from those found by Indians in northern Wisconsin or on the shores of Lake Michigan and Lake Superior.

18   **reunite:** To meet again after being separated   **peak:** The highest point

For example, archaeologists think that the Archaic Indians who lived in the southwestern part of the state moved into the small river valleys of the Driftless Area in winter. They could easily hunt the deer that gathered in these valleys.

Meanwhile, Archaic people in the glaciated parts of Wisconsin used the resources around lakes. The Indians caught turtles, fish, ducks, and other waterfowl as they camped during the warmer months. These different hunting **strategies** (**strat** uh jeez) helped Archaic groups gather large amounts of food and prepare for winter.

Archaic arrowhead

No matter where they lived, Archaic people developed a relationship to the land. Archaic Indians felt attached to places where they expected to return. These were places where their grandparents had lived, died, and were now buried. These were the places they expected their children to live. The Archaic people created traditions that linked them to particular pieces of land.

Just like today, people valued cemeteries because family members were buried there. Cemeteries connect those who lived in the past to those who come after them. Archaeologists have found **evidence** of cemeteries from the Archaic period. They know that people returned to these cemeteries **generation** after generation. Cemeteries were **sacred** (**say** krid) or special to Archaic groups. Many families today feel the same way about cemeteries where their **ancestors** (**an** ses turz) are buried.

Starting about 2,800 years ago, other groups of Indians followed the Archaic Indians in Wisconsin. These groups lived in what archaeologists call the Woodland era. Woodland Indians are the **descendants** (di **sen** duhnts) of Archaic Indians.

strategies: Plans **evidence:** Material that helps prove something really happened **generation:** A group of descendants from a shared ancestor who are alive at the same time **sacred:** Deserving of respect **ancestors:** Family members from long ago **descendants:** Someone's children and grandchildren and their children and grandchildren

This pottery piece was once part of a jar used by Woodland Indians.

Wisconsin Historical Museum 1994.287.
DA736.F.110-S-1

Archaeologists have learned from the clues that Woodland Indians left behind that these groups felt attached to particular places where they buried their dead, just as Archaic Indians did.

Remember that Paleo-Indians, Archaic Indians, and Woodland Indians were not all members of the same tribe. They didn't all speak the same language or live in the same place or places. But archaeologists have learned that Indian groups living in Wisconsin during the same time period developed similar ways of doing things.

For example, Woodland Indians buried their dead in different ways than did Archaic Indians. You can see some of these burial grounds even today. Some Woodland people introduced new ways of shaping the land—farming and mound building.

The Meaning of Mounds

The mound-building traditions of Wisconsin's Woodland Indians grew out of their religious ideas. People buried their dead in mounds of various shapes. Some of their mounds were large domes. Others were long and straight, or **linear** (**lin** ee ur). Still others were in the shapes of humans, animal, or spirits like water panthers and thunderbirds. We call this last group **effigy** (**ef** uh jee) **mounds**.

WHi Image ID 78519

Bear effigy near Lake Koshkonong

20   **linear:** Long, like a pencil   **effigy mounds:** Indian mounds carved in the shape of an animal

Mounds were more than just places to bury the dead. Mound building and the mounds themselves meant many things to the groups who built them. Woodland people created mounds to express religious or **spiritual** (**spir** uh choo uhl) beliefs. Mound builders also used mounds to mark **boundaries**.

Building the mounds and carrying out **ceremonies** (**ser** uh moh neez) or festivals around them helped bring a community closer together. More than 20,000 mounds of various shapes once covered Wisconsin's landscape. Nearly all of them were still there when non-Indian settlers began to arrive in the late 1600s.

Woodland Indians built most of their effigy mounds on ridges or bluffs overlooking rivers and lakes. They also built them along main travel routes. When you visit effigy mound sites today, be sure to look where the mound builders placed their mounds in the landscape.

Human activities like plowing destroyed most Wisconsin mounds. A smaller number of

Amelia Janes, Earth Illustrated, Inc.

Lake Mendota
Effigy Mounds

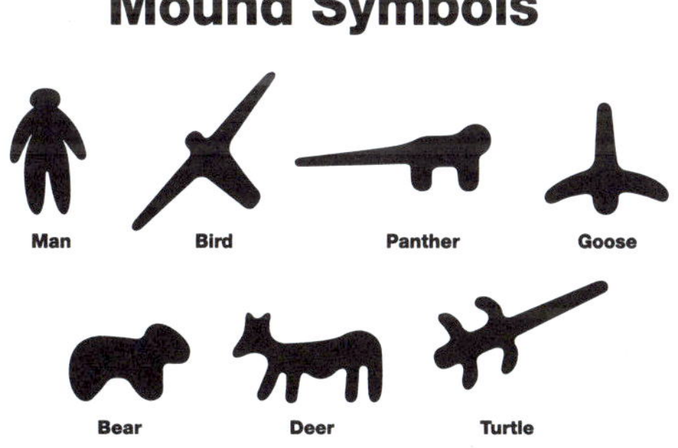

Mound Symbols

spiritual: Having to do with the soul   **boundaries:** The lines that separate one area from another
ceremonies: Important acts done at special times and places

mounds were destroyed by natural **processes** like **soil erosion** (i **roh** zhuhn). Since 1987, state laws protect the mounds as a special part of Wisconsin's landscape.

The First Farmers

Mounds are not the only evidence you can see today of the way Woodland Indians changed Wisconsin's landscape before **Europeans** (yur up **pee** uhns) arrived. The changes to the land made by these early Indians helped them produce larger amounts of food.

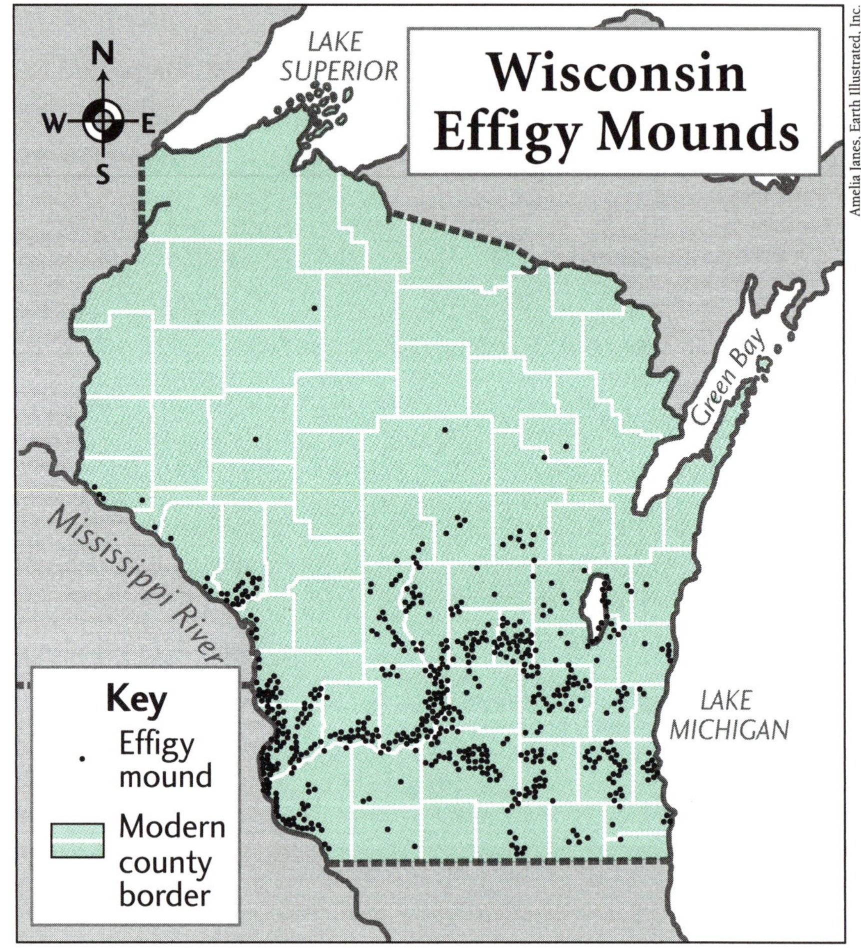

processes: Series of actions that produce a result **soil erosion:** The wearing away of soil by water or air
Europeans: People from the continent of Europe

For example, early Indians used fire to clear land and to create **habitats** (**hab** uh tats) that attracted deer, elk, and **game** birds like wild turkeys. Early Indians even used fire to drive game into particular areas that made hunting easier. Burning the grass often helped Indians increase the amounts of blueberries, acorns, and nuts that they could harvest.

Woodland Indians were also the first to **cultivate** or farm the land they lived on. Catholic **missionary** (**mish** uh ner ee) Father Jacques Marquette (**zhok** mhar **ket**) described the **groves** of plum trees and grapevines between the prairies and cornfields that he saw in 1673 when he arrived in southeast Wisconsin. Indian groups in the southern part of the state were also growing squash, beans, and corn. These three foods formed the basic crops of the Americas before the Europeans arrived.

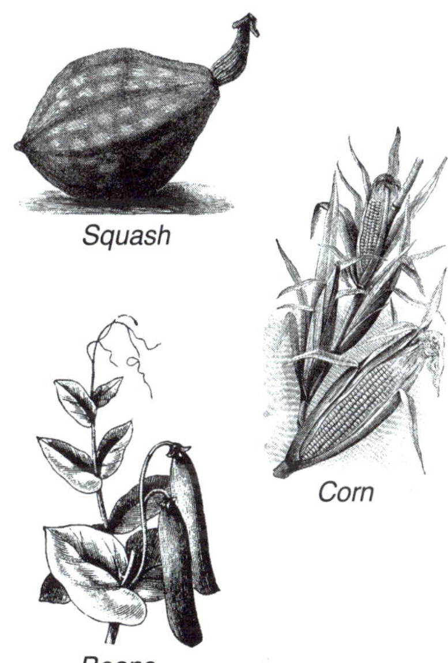

Squash

Corn

Beans

Some Woodland Indian groups were **innovative** (**in** uh vay tiv) in their farming. The Woodland Indians planted their crops in raised, ridged fields. The ridges protected the crops planted *between* them from frost damage during cold weather. By building ridges, early Indian gardeners increased the length of the growing season.

---

habitats: Places and natural conditions where plants and animals live **game:** Wild animals that are hunted for sport and food **cultivate:** To plant, grow, and harvest **missionary:** Someone who is sent by a church or religious group to teach the group's faith **groves:** Groups of trees growing or planted near one another **innovative:** Inventing new ways of doing things

Planting in the same place year after year often wears out the soil. That's why Woodland Indians **rotated** the planting of their gardens. That is, they changed the location of the gardens each season. They let one piece of ground rest between planting seasons. This practice helped make the soil produce better crops. The Oneota (oh nee **oh** tuh) tribe also used garbage to enrich the soil similar to the way people use **compost** (**kahm** pohst) today.

These ridged garden beds show how the ancestors of the Ho-Chunk raised crops in Wisconsin long ago.

Various groups of Indians throughout Wisconsin continued to locate their homes near wetlands and river bottoms. These locations allowed people to take advantage of the large variety of fish, shellfish, birds, animals, and plant resources there. Early Indian groups in the southern half of Wisconsin also preferred settling on land "on the edge," which meant settling on land between prairie and forest.

Non-Indian settlers who later arrived in southern Wisconsin also tended to settle the land "on the edge" for the same reasons. Everyone realized they needed the fertile grassland of the prairies for **agriculture** (**ag** ruh kul chur) and nearby wood from the forest for building and fuel.

rotated: Switched from season to season   **compost:** A mixture of dead leaves, grass, and food waste that is added to soil to make it richer   **agriculture:** Farming

The early Indian groups living here before the Europeans arrived enjoyed the natural resources of Wisconsin's environment. These early people also took only what they needed from the land. But as you have learned, they also made changes to the land by using fire, planting crops, and building effigy mounds.

Non-Indians began arriving around the year 1700. After Europeans arrived, changes to the landscape—and to Native communities—increased much more rapidly.

Chapter 3

The Fur Trade Brings
New Ways of Living

◆ ◆ ◆

The **technology** (tek **nol** oh jee) created in the twentieth century completely changed the lives of everyone in Wisconsin and around the world. Your great-great-grandparents probably did not travel by airplane. Your great-grandparents probably grew up without television. Even though your grandparents could listen to the radio or watch television when they were young, they couldn't listen to a popular song on a computer. Your parents may have used computers when they were growing up, but the internet was not widely used the way it is today.

U.S. Senator Bob La Follette and his family seated around a radio in 1924

Over the last 100 years, people have accepted these inventions. It seems that people now seem to expect rapid change in the way we live, work, and travel.

 technology: The use of science and engineering to do practical things

In the last chapter, you learned how Indians in Wisconsin shaped the land before Europeans came to North America. About 400 years ago, 2 events created major changes for the people living in what is now Wisconsin. First, Europeans arrived in North America. Second, the **fur trade** began in the Great Lakes region.

The first Europeans arrived in the 1600s. They were explorers, fur traders, and missionaries.

Europeans learned from Indians. Indians learned from Europeans. The Europeans learned much about the land and the habits of the animals from the Indians who were already here. Wisconsin Indians learned from the Europeans about new tools and ideas about how the world worked.

This **exchange** between Indians and Europeans created a new series of events that forever changed how land was used in Wisconsin—and who controlled it.

Think About It

How were Wisconsin Indians using the land at the time the Europeans arrived? How did the exchange between Indians and Europeans completely transform the way people here used the land and its resources? Why was the fur trade so important? How did Indian life in Wisconsin change as a result of the fur trade?

Wisconsin Indian Traditions

Many Indian nations were living in the area when Europeans arrived here in the late 1600s. The 3 main groups were the Ho-Chunk, the Menominee (muh **nah** muh nee), and the Dakota.

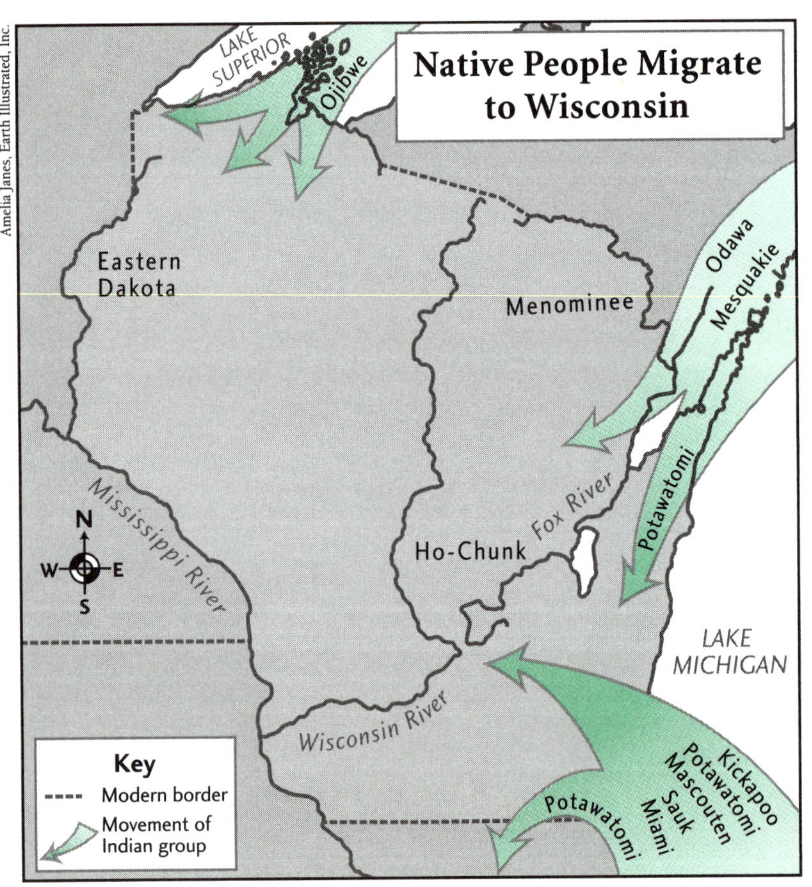

The Ho-Chunk and Menominee people remained in Wisconsin. Both nations continue to live here today. But the Dakota have long since moved west of the Mississippi into present-day Minnesota.

Other Indian people in Wisconsin in the 1600s included the Potawatomi (pah tuh **wah** tuh mee), Ojibwe (oh **jib** wah), Kickapoo, Sauk (sawk), Mesquakie (mes **kwaw** kee) (or Fox), Mascouten (muh **skoo** tuhn), Ioway, and Miami. Like the Ho-Chunk and Menominee, the Potawatomi and Ojibwe still live here today.

Wisconsin's Indian people survived as they had long before Europeans arrived. That is, Indians continued to hunt, fish, grow vegetables, and gather foods like cranberries and wild rice. The natural environment supplied their basic needs, just as it had for their ancestors. Indian people were able to take care of themselves and their families by using natural resources. It was not difficult for a group of Indian families to search for an area with better resources and move there.

This Indian village near Green Bay was home to the Menominee.

The Native groups that got along shared ideas, tools, and traditions. Some even traded with groups from other parts of Wisconsin. The Indian groups that didn't get along with others most often disagreed about land. They fought over areas with the best natural resources: berries, wild rice, good hunting and fishing, and good soil for corn, beans, and squash.

Living with the Land

How different Indian groups lived still depended on *where* they lived and on the resources in that particular area. By the time Europeans arrived, Indian groups in different parts of Wisconsin had created different patterns of everyday living.

The Ojibwe and others living in the forests near Lake Superior were **nomadic** (noh **mad** ik). They moved around during the year to take advantage of the best areas to hunt, fish, and gather wild rice.

nomadic: Moving from place to place to survive

The Ojibwe still harvest wild rice today.

Three Ojibwe Indians gather wild rice from a canoe.

Deer meat, fish, and wild rice were the most important foods in the diet of the Indians in northern Wisconsin. But these groups also **tapped** maple trees for sap in the spring and planted small vegetable gardens. This far north, the growing season was very short.

In the summer, large groups of several tribal bands lived along the coast of Lake Superior in homes made of birch bark. In the winter, the food supply was low and game was scarce. It was harder for large groups to find enough resources to feed everyone, so large groups of Ojibwe members broke into smaller bands. Then they moved deeper into the forest, where they were more protected from the weather and more likely to find the food and shelter they needed.

The smaller bands of Ojibwe rebuilt their birch-bark **lodges** in their winter locations. They covered the lodges with branches of cedar to keep the people inside warm. Living in smaller groups meant that they could make limited resources last longer.

The growing season was slightly longer in the region of northeastern Wisconsin where the

    tapped: Made a hole to draw out a liquid, such as sap from a tree   **lodges:** Indian homes or dwellings

Menominee, or "wild rice people," lived. Like the Ojibwe, they hunted, fished, and gathered wild rice. They harvested corn, beans, and pumpkins in the area close to Lake Winnebago. But wild rice and fish remained more important.

The Menominee were **stationary**. They did not have to move around to find resources. The Menominee lived in large villages. In the summer, they lived in dome-shaped lodges covered with bark or **reed** mats. In the winter, they lived in rectangular bark lodges, which were warmer.

The Ho-Chunk and other groups in southern Wisconsin had the longest growing season. They were able to raise corn, beans, and squash. Their fields of vegetables supplied their main foods, even though Ho-Chunk members also hunted and fished. These Indians of southwestern Wisconsin did not have to move around. Like their Menominee neighbors to the northeast, the Ho-Chunk people lived in large villages.

A Menominee family dressed in traditional clothing, 1931

Sometimes the Menominee hunters would join Ho-Chunk hunters to search for buffalo farther west. Like the Menominee, the Ho-Chunk people built their homes of bark in winter. In summer, the Ho-Chunk built their homes of reed mats and sturdy grasses.

These patterns of land use continued after Europeans brought the fur trade to Wisconsin. But Indian life soon grew much more complicated. The fur trade was at the center of these changes.

The Fur Trade

For hundreds of years, Indian people in the Great Lakes region had hunted fur-bearing animals for food and clothing. They hunted for mink, otter, and beaver. Beaver was especially **plentiful**.

Europeans also found beaver **pelts** to be perfect material to make felt hats. Felt hats were very popular among wealthy men in Europe at that time. Indian hunters could provide the beaver pelts that Europeans valued so highly.

As long as felt hats were popular, European **hatters** wanted all the pelts they could get. The French Canadians **managed** much of the fur trade The French Canadians delivered the furs from the Indian beaver hunters to the French **manufacturers** of European hats.

Ho-Chunk brothers Frank and Henry Winneshiek (**wi** nuh shek) in traditional clothing, 1884

WHi Image ID 61113

plentiful: Existing in large amounts   **pelts:** Animals skins with the fur or hair still on them   **hatters:** People who make hats
managed: Took charge of   **manufacturers:** Companies that make something

European idea of beavers at work, 1711

A beaver making a dam

Indian family roles changed when families began to produce food and fur for trade rather than for their own needs. Women had played important roles in preparing beaver pelts for clothing or food for their families. Now, they spent much of their time cleaning and preparing the furs for trading.

This hat was created from beaver pelts.

Europeans brought new goods to the Great Lakes to exchange for the pelts. These new materials included brass kettles and knives, cloth for clothing, blankets, and glass beads.

Many members of Indian groups chose to supply the furs so that they could trade furs for these goods. Trade now became central to Indian life. Indian people had

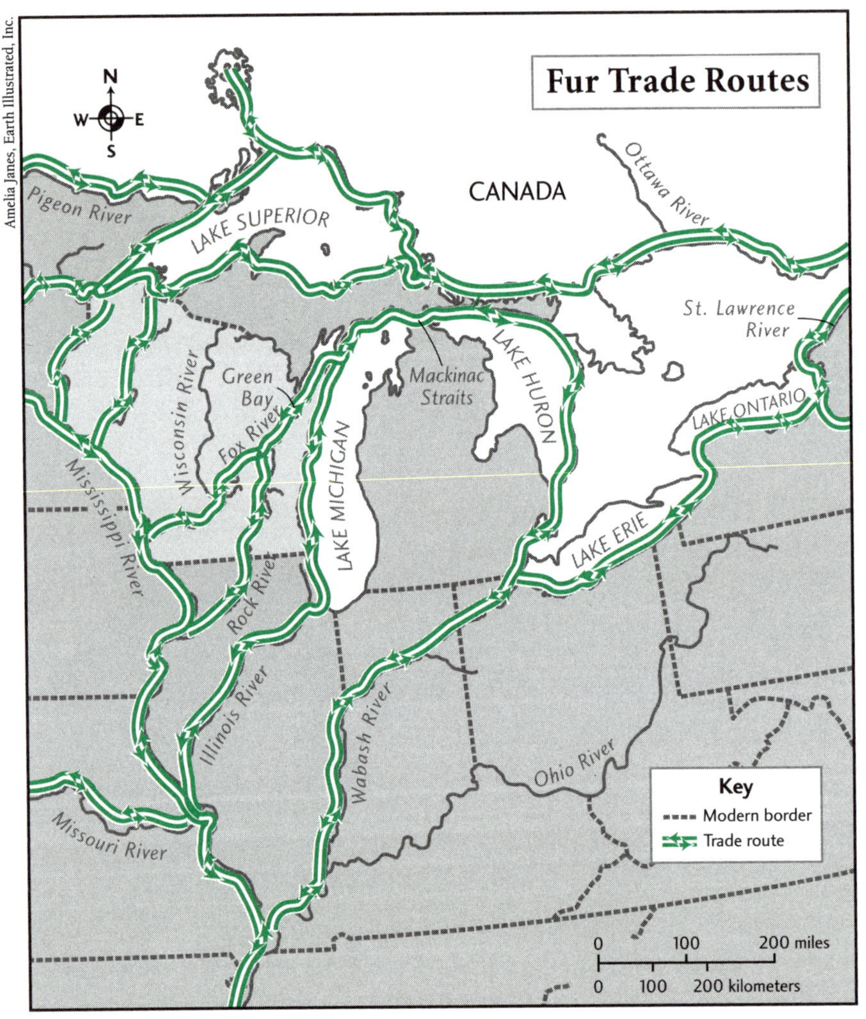

been **independent**, living off the land and its resources, before Europeans arrived. Now, their **livelihood** (**lɪv** lee hud) depended on Europeans.

Some Indian people in Wisconsin welcomed trade goods that made life easier. They enjoyed using brass kettles for cooking, metal knives for hunting and scraping furs, and woolen fabrics for clothing.

Members of tribal groups did not give up their own traditions, however. They chose to **modify** (**mod** uh fī) them by adding new materials and

independent: Free of the control of other people or things **livelihood:** Way of making enough money to support oneself
modify: To change a little

tools. But once they began trading for goods, Indians became **dependent** on the Europeans. Now Indians were trapping beaver to exchange for European goods. Living off the land was no longer enough.

New Attitudes

During the fur trade era many Indian men *had* to kill enough beaver to be able to trade with the Europeans. These men now hunted many more beaver than they needed for their own families. Soon the hunters killed off the beaver population near their homes.

Indian hunters had to hunt for beaver farther and farther away. Hunting farther from home meant that the men had to be away from their families for longer periods.

Hunting beaver in winter was not easy. It meant cutting a hole in the ice of a beaver pond, putting **bait** in the hole, and then waiting until a beaver appeared.

The hunter had to be extremely patient. When the beaver came to take the bait, the hunter clubbed the beaver. This method worked well for catching a single beaver, enough for one family's needs. Once Indians became involved with the fur trade, they needed to catch beaver more **efficiently** .

Madeline Island Museum #83.237.375

Beads from France were used to decorate this Ojibwe pouch from 1780. How do you think the Ojibwe people got the beads?

dependent: Controlled by other people or things **bait:** Food used to attract something to be caught
efficiently: Working without wasting time

WHi Image ID 35238

This home was owned by the DuCharme family in Kaukauna and used as a fur trading post.

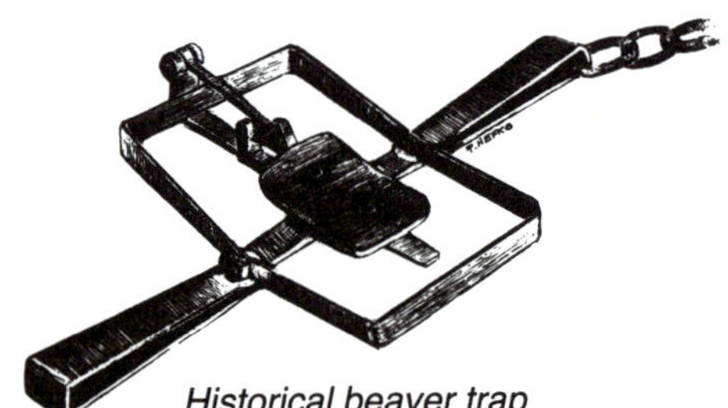
Historical beaver trap

By 1750, Indian hunters caught beaver using traps supplied by the fur traders. They baited the traps with a mixture of spices. The Indian trappers learned this method from Europeans, and it worked well.

Many Indian people involved in the fur trade moved their families away from their villages to be closer to the trading posts in these towns. As a result, traditional Indian communities grew smaller.

Their relationship to the land and its resources also changed. Beaver had been one of the key resources that Indians had taken from the land. By the early 1800s, the supply of beaver was very low.

Amelia Janes, Earth Illustrated, Inc.

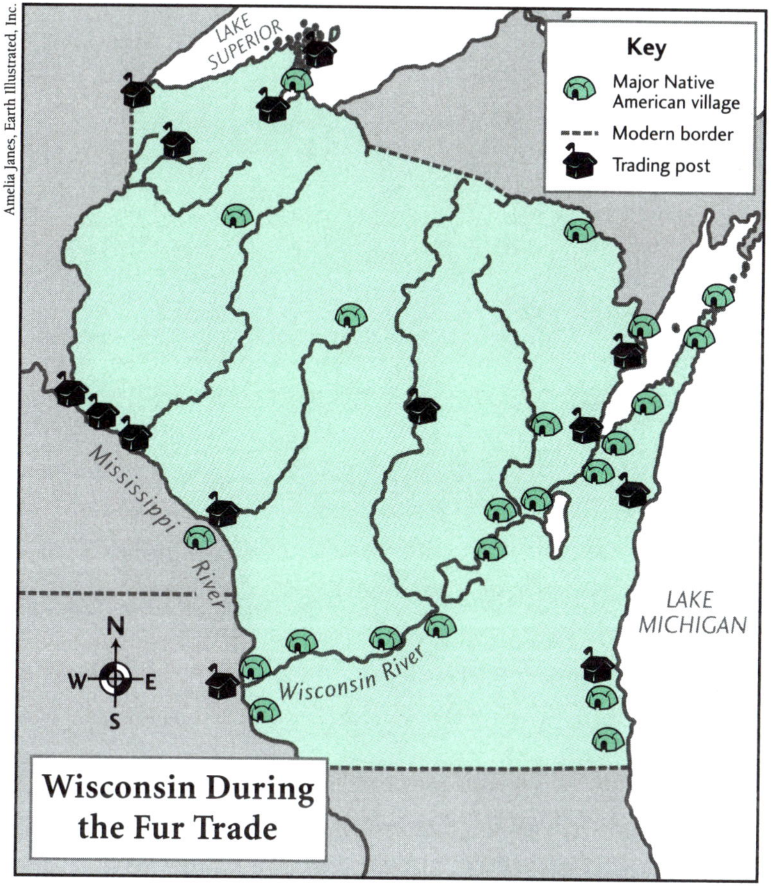

Wisconsin During the Fur Trade

Europeans and Indians were now dealing with the land and its resources in ways that Indians had not known before the fur trade. Now Indians were not simply living off the land.

Trade had brought Indians new goods that they enjoyed using, but trade also had brought a new way of living. This new way of living and using land and its resources was not always good for the land, for the plants and animals, or for Wisconsin's Indian people.

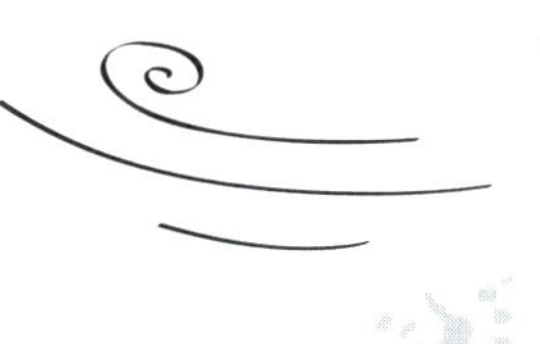

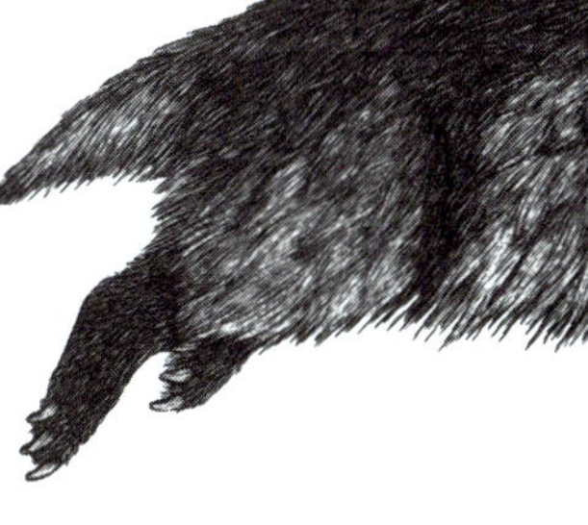

Chapter 4

Treaty Making and Land Taking

◆ ◆ ◆

Imagine you hit a **double** in a baseball game and are standing on second base. Your team has no outs, and you're excited about your chances of being able to score a run. But when the next player strikes out, you are told that your team is no longer at bat. Suddenly, the rules have changed—right in the middle of the game! Instead of 3 outs to end the inning, your team only gets 1. You have no idea what happened or why.

Now, imagine you are in the middle of a 30-minute math test. After 13 minutes, your teacher announces, "Time's up!" You look down at your paper. You're not even halfway done! Why did your teacher choose to switch the time and not bother to let the students know? Both of these situations are unfair.

Something similar happened to Wisconsin's Indian people during the 1800s. Only the results were much worse. Tribal people had their own **cultures** and their own rules. Traditional ways of making a living and relating to the world and their neighbors now changed forever.

---

   double: A hit that earns the hitter 2 bases in baseball   **culture:** The way of life, ideas, and traditions of a group of people

Indian people in Wisconsin had known Europeans through the fur trade. Indians had worked and often lived with Europeans on traditional tribal homelands. But this way of life disappeared when the fur trade ended at the end of the 1700s.

The people of Wisconsin had reached another turning point in their history. Beginning in the early 1800s, new groups of non-Indian settlers began to move into the area to take control of Wisconsin's land and resources. Tribal people now had to make new and larger **adaptations** (ad ap **tay** shuhns) in order to survive.

The United States government began making **treaties** with Wisconsin Indian nations. It was as if the rules of the game suddenly changed. Treaties changed Indian life in Wisconsin forever. You'll find out why in this chapter.

Think About It

What changes to Indian life did new settlement bring? What role did lead mining play in these changes? How was the Black Hawk War a turning point for both Indians and new settlers? How did the signing of treaties affect Wisconsin Indians? How did it affect new settlers? How did the signing of treaties lead to Wisconsin becoming a U.S. **territory**?

1852 drawing of a Ho-Chunk **ciiporoke** (chi **poh** tohk ay), or wigwam

This drawing shows the Ojibwe performing the traditional pipe dance and tomahawk dance at the signing of the 1825 treaty in Prairie du Chien.

adaptations: Acts of changing to fit a new situation   **treaties:** Agreements between nations   **territory:** An area that a nation owns but does not call a state

Treaties and Trouble

How do treaties work? Two or more nations **negotiate** (nig **oh** shee ayt) treaties when they need to agree on something important—such as ending a war, trading goods, or using land.

The individuals who sign these **official** agreements sign for their nation. Each nation promises to stand by the agreement and to **conduct** official business by following what the treaty says.

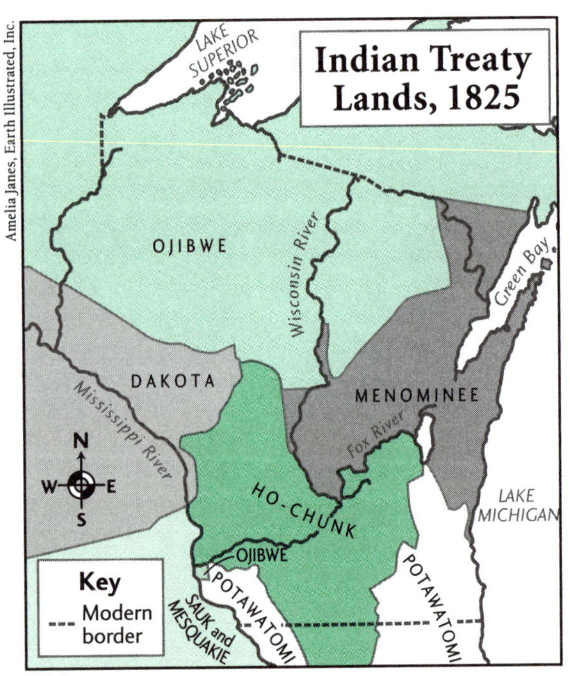

Amelia Janes, Earth Illustrated, Inc.

Treaty making is always complicated. Treaties between North American Indian groups and the government of the United States had to do with land use and landownership. These treaties led to bitter misunderstandings. The U.S. government created the treaties. Treaty-making was familiar to them, but not to the Indian groups with whom the U.S. government negotiated.

There were great differences in the attitudes of tribal people and the U.S. government when it came to land use. There were also great differences in how Native and non-Native groups understood one another.

  negotiate: Discuss something in order to come to an agreement   **official:** Respected by an authority
conduct: To carry out; do

You've learned how the fur trade changed some traditions that tribal people followed. The fur trade encouraged Indian groups to use up some of the land's natural resources, such as beavers. But no one asked the tribal groups to move from or give up their homelands.

Dealing with the U.S. government was very different. Unlike the fur traders, American settlers were not interested in only taking resources from the land. They wanted to lay claim to the land itself and settle permanently. The first step in the process was working out a treaty with some willing tribal members. But what would make an Indian tribe willing to give up its right to the land?

Native people had worked with Europeans for more than 150 years during the fur trade period. Then the area in which they lived came under the control of the government of the United States. In the early 1800s, Indian people understood that the U.S. government wanted to use their land. But most tribal groups did not realize that signing a treaty with the government meant *giving up* their own rights to use the land *forever.*

Many Indian groups could not understand how or why they needed to give up their homelands. The treaties meant exchanging land for *payment.* The very idea went against Indian traditions. These traditions taught that land was a gift of the Great Spirit. Tribal members believed that no person or people could own

This portrait of an Ojibwe woman with her child on her back was painted in 1826.

land. Indian people did not understand the idea of permanently buying or selling land. From the tribal point of view, land ownership itself did not make sense. Treaty-making **disrupted** (dis **ruhp** ted) Indians' traditional ways of living and controlling their own lives.

Treaties were official forms of agreement, but they were unfair to the Indian groups signing them. What made them unfair? First, the treaties were written in English, the language of the U.S. officials. These officials wanted to make a treaty that would allow the government to take over tribal homelands, but that was not always clear to the Indians.

The United States of America, have seen with much regret that wars have, for many years been carried on between the Sioux and the Chippewas; and more recently between the confederated tribes of Sacs and Foxes, and the Sioux: and also between the Ioways and Sioux; which if not terminated may extend to the other tribes, and involve the Indians, upon the Missouri, the Mississippi and the Lakes, in general hostilities. In order therefore to promote peace, among these tribes. and to establish boundaries among them, and the other tribes; who live in their vicinity, and thereby to remove all causes of future difficulty The United States, have invited the Chippewa, Sac & Fox, Menominee Ioway, Sioux, Winnebago And a portion of the Ottawa Chippewa and Potawatomie tribes of Indians

WHi Image ID 43574

What Indian tribe names can you see in the 1825 treaty?

Second, officials who tried to explain the treaties to the Indians had trouble because they did not always know the tribal language. Unfortunately, some officials also made the treaty language unclear on purpose. Those officials hoped that tribal members would be willing to sign without fully understanding the long-lasting **consequences** (**kahn** suh kwen sez) of the agreement.

    disrupted: Got in the way of; interrupted   **consequences:** Effects

Some tribes had **elders** or leaders who met in **councils** to make decisions. U.S. officials sometimes ignored or made no effort to find these leaders. Instead, these officials looked for tribal members willing to sign to gain more money or goods for themselves. Often, these tribal members were willing to negotiate with the U.S. government. But they did not have the **authority** to sign for their tribe.

Unfortunately, other members of that nation had to live with the results once the treaties had been signed. After all, the United States was much larger and more powerful.

The dishonesty in the treaty-making process led to anger and distrust. Often the United States never delivered the money or goods promised in exchange for Indian lands. Sometimes the government promised the tribes land farther west that belonged to Indian groups already living there.

Sometimes the new land did not have the natural resources necessary for the group to live well. Some groups, like the Ho-Chunk, were forced to move again and again. These journeys were very difficult, especially for young children and older people. Tribal members lost more than their homelands. They lost the ability to provide for their families.

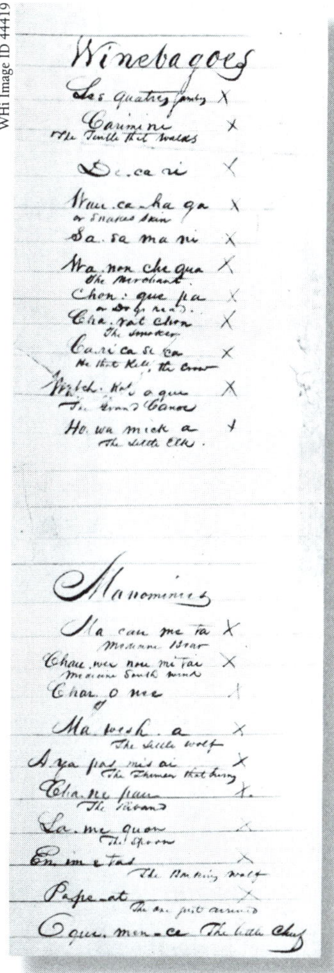

The Indians who signed the 1825 Treaty signed their names with an "X."

elders: Respected older leaders **councils:** Groups of people who discuss and make decisions **authority:** Power

Before Black Hawk

Understanding the difficulties caused by treaty making helps explain why the Treaty of 1804 was the beginning of a major conflict with major consequences. This treaty was between some members of the Sauk and Mesquakie nations and the United States government. It was the first treaty signed by Indian nations from Wisconsin and the United States. The Treaty of 1804 led to the Black Hawk War nearly 30 years later.

American settlers were just beginning to push west from the East Coast and settle on the land in the Midwest when the Treaty of 1804 was signed. This treaty allowed the Sauk and Mesquakie people to farm the land *as long as it was owned by the U.S. government*. But just a few years after signing the treaty, the U.S. government would sell the land to new settlers. Once the settlers moved in, the Sauk and Mesquakie would be forced to leave their homelands. The Indians did not know that the treaty they had signed meant they would **eventually** have to give up their land and move away.

From 1812 through 1815, Great Britain and the United States fought a war for control of the region west of the Great Lakes. The United States won. At that time the United States was growing as more Americans were born, and more Europeans immigrated to make the United States their home. Many of these people chose to move west.

As settlers moved west, the number of states and territories **expanded** . Since the U.S. government knew that individual settlers would want to buy land, it signed treaties that would make land available for this fast-growing country. About 1820, these settlers began to arrive in the area around the western Great Lakes. These

 eventually: At a time in the future   **expanded:** Grew in number

settlers' need for land is behind the **tragic** story of Black Hawk.

On the Lookout for Lead

Around 1820, non-Indians from all over the United States began to move to and settle in what later became the state of Wisconsin. No longer did the promise of trading furs draw people to the Great Lakes. The land in what is now southwest Wisconsin, northeastern Iowa, and northwestern Illinois contained rich deposits of a soft, grey mineral known as **galena** (guh **lee** nuh). Galena is the source of lead (led).

In 1825, the United States invited the Ojibwe, Dakota, and other Indian nations to meet at Prairie du Chien to sign the treaty that became the first step in getting these tribes to give up their lands.

Lead drew the first large numbers of U.S. citizens and European **immigrants** to the region. These new arrivals hoped to make their fortunes mining lead in the part of the Driftless Area between the Mississippi, Sugar, and Wisconsin rivers.

When we hear about lead today, it is mostly in terms of lead poisoning. We know that in some forms, lead can endanger the lives of animals and humans. But in the 1800s, people were not completely aware of these dangers. Lead was a very valuable mineral.

tragic: Sad and dramatic   **galena:** A shiny gray mineral used to make lead   **immigrants:** People who move to a new area from another country

Manufacturers used lead to make things that a fast-growing country like the United States needed: **lead shot**, roofing and gutters, pipes, weights, toys, **printers' type**, and paint.

The Ho-Chunk, Sauk, Mesquakie, and other Indian nations had mined lead in southwest Wisconsin for thousands of years. They used lead to make jewelry and paint. They were mining lead even before the 1600s when French explorers had first entered the region.

Indian lead miners also traded lead to the Europeans. Europeans used lead shot as **ammunition** (am yoo **nish** uhn). As they had for beaver, the Indians began to spend more time and energy producing greater amounts of lead for trade.

Indian women mined the lead, and older men carried it back to the surface.

The Indian lead miners were women. They scooped up the lead that lay just beneath the surface of the land. Or they dug tunnels and **shafts** to mine larger amounts of lead. When the lead was mined in one area, the miners left these "diggings" behind to look for lead elsewhere. U.S. settlers arrived in the 1820s. They found the "diggings" of these Indian miners. Most of the Indian miners still lived in the area.

Over the years, the Ho-Chunk, Sauk, Mesquakie, and other people living in southwest Wisconsin had allowed a few non-Indians to mine. Under the terms of the 1804 treaty, the U.S. government could invite

 lead shot: Small pellets used in guns before bullets were invented   **printers' type:** Metal letters used to print in early printing machines   **ammunition:** Material shot out of guns   **shafts:** Tunnels going straight down into the ground

settlers to **lease**—but not buy—land in order to dig for lead. Indian groups who had been living in the area for many generations did not know that the arrival of these new miners would eventually force Native people to leave.

Ho-Chunk elder Spoon Decorah remembered that when settlers began to dig for lead, they promised to supply the Indians with lead. But the settlers broke their promises. "We never saw any of our lead again, except what we paid dearly for," Spoon Decorah complained, "and we never will have any given to us, unless it be fired at us out of white men's guns, to kill us off."

Ebenezer Brigham (eb uh **nee** zur **brig** uhm) was the first non-Indian settler in what became Dane County. He met with his Ho-Chunk neighbors at Blue Mounds to set a boundary between Ho-Chunk land and his diggings. This boundary line protected the **claims** of both the Ho-Chunk nation and Brigham. He told one of his friends how tribal members " **blazed** the trees along this line" so that whites would know not to pass beyond it and mine Ho-Chunk land.

lease: To rent for a period of time   **sulfur:** An element used in gunpowder, matches, and fertilizer
evaporates: Turns from liquid to gas   **claims:** Rights to ownership   **blazed:** Burned

Brigham also operated a trading post where Ho-Chunk members living around Blue Mounds did business. He wrote several Ho-Chunk words at the back of his **ledger** to help him communicate with his Indian customers in their own language.

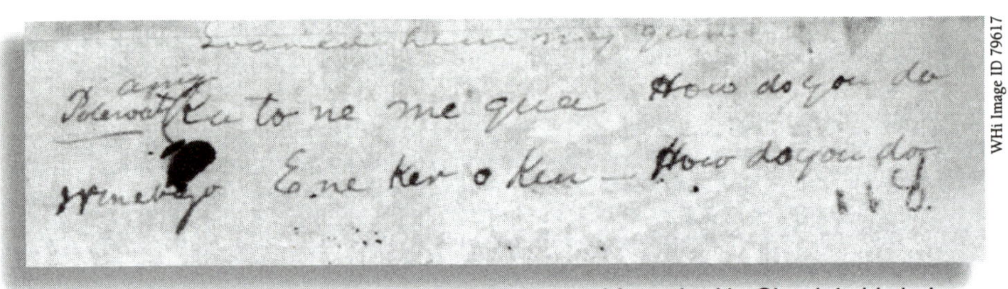
Ebenezer Brigham wrote down the words he learned from the Ho-Chunk in his ledger.

By 1825, most of the lead once found on the surface of the land was gone. Indians and non-Indian miners like Brigham now had to sink a mining shaft deep into the ground. Brigham built a **smelter** nearby to melt down the lead. Blue Mounds was becoming a real settlement.

Many others coming to work in the lead mines began settling in places such as Potosi, Shullsburg, Hardscrabble, New Diggings, and Mineral Point. Farmers followed. Conflicts arose as the Indians began to realize that these newcomers had come not to visit but to *stay*. The newcomers' settlements **threatened** the Indians' way of life.

Tribal members mined lead and continued to plant large fields of corn, beans, and squash. Indian groups still moved regularly to hunt and to gather plants that ripened at particular times of year. These Indian groups needed the *freedom* to move around the area in order to use the land in the same ways they always had.

But the new settlers failed to understand how Indians could consider land *theirs* when they only used it for part of the year. As more settlers moved to the area, it became

   ledger: Book where money related to a business is written down   **smelter:** A place where metal is melted
threatened: Put in danger

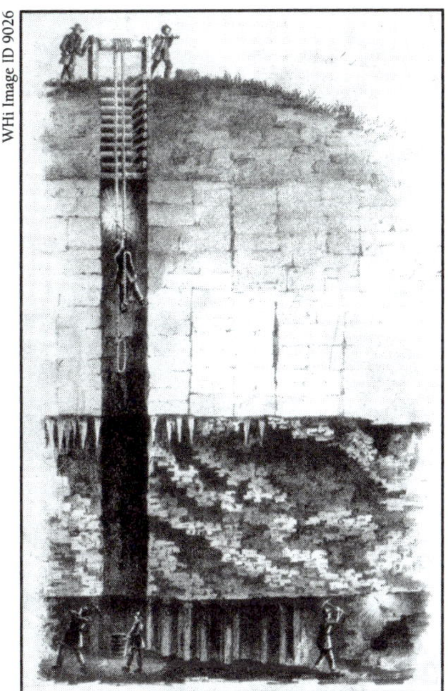
This drawing shows how deep miners dug shafts for lead.

more and more difficult for tribal people to continue their way of life. When these non-Indians settled on particular pieces of land, they were unwilling to allow tribal members to use it for their seasonal activities like planting, harvesting, hunting, and fishing. Tribal people did not understand or accept the American point of view that land could be owned by individuals. Unfortunately, this difference in ideas about land use increased. So did the conflicts between settlers and the region's Indian groups.

The Black Hawk War

Chief Black Hawk in 1832

Black Hawk was a Sauk Indian leader from the area where the Rock River flows into the Mississippi. His actions brought conflicts between Indians and settlers in the area to a head. His **protest**, unfortunately, led to what became known as the Black Hawk War. The results of the Black Hawk War forever changed land use in Wisconsin.

In 1828, the U.S. government decided to sell the Indian lands it had gained through the Treaty of 1804. The government warned the leaders of different Sauk and Mesquakie groups that they would have to leave their villages on the eastern bank of the Mississippi River by spring. These Indians were being forced to move to the western bank of the Mississippi River in what is now Iowa. Some of the people agreed.

protest: Strong public disagreement

But Black Hawk and his band claimed that the order was **unjust**. The move would not allow enough time for his followers to harvest the corn they had planted. The Indians depended upon the harvested corn for their winter food supply. The U.S. government promised to deliver plenty of food for winter. Black Hawk's people moved as they were told. But the promised food from the U.S. government never arrived. Black Hawk's anger grew as his people suffered and starved.

In April 1832, Black Hawk and about 1,200 followers—families of men, women, and children—returned to their old villages in what is now Illinois. They crossed to the eastern bank of the Mississippi River near the mouth of the Rock River. When they arrived, the Indians found that settlers had planted corn in areas the Sauk and Mesquakie people had once farmed.

Black Hawk knew he could do nothing but return to their villages on the west bank of the Mississippi. But the settlers feared problems with the Indians who had returned to the east bank of the river. Many of the male settlers formed a **militia** (muh **lish** uh) to protect their communities.

Black Hawk understood that he and his band were not welcome to stay in their old villages on the east bank of the Mississippi River. He also knew that he and his followers were greatly outnumbered. His followers were not warriors. They were hungry families searching for food. Black Hawk was ready to **surrender** to the militia. He sent several men with a white flag of peace.

But some militia members misunderstood. They panicked and fired their rifles. These militia members killed some of Black Hawk's peacemakers. The Black Hawk War began when the surviving Indians fired back in self-defense.

  unjust: Not fair   **militia:** A volunteer army   **surrender:** To give up

Black Hawk wanted to lead his people back across the Mississippi, but the militia blocked the way. Black Hawk hoped to cross the Mississippi further north, so he and his followers headed up the Rock River into Wisconsin.

Black Hawk tried to keep his followers safe, but traveling with families was slow. Black Hawk needed to keep the troops from striking the main group of his people. He also needed to get food for his people. Black Hawk sent out small groups to **raid** frontier farms and villages in the lead-mining district. Settlers there were frightened. Some, like Ebenezer Brigham at Blue Mounds, built a **fort** .

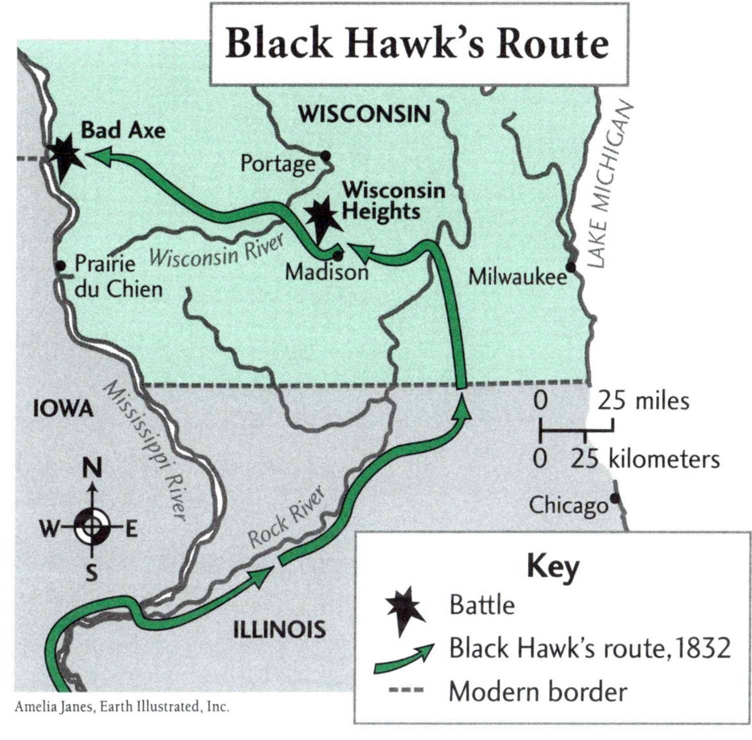

Amelia Janes, Earth Illustrated, Inc.

Meanwhile, Black Hawk and the rest of his band kept heading northwest toward the Wisconsin River. They knew they could follow that large river west to the Mississippi. Black Hawk expected more help from the British or other Indian groups. That help never came. But the U.S. Army came to help the militia. Even the Native people who agreed with Black Hawk did not want to fight the U.S. Army.

raid: To take with force   **fort:** A building built strong enough to survive attacks, sometimes surrounded by walls or tall fences

This is how an artist named Cal Peters imagined Black Hawk's surrender. He painted this picture in 1940.

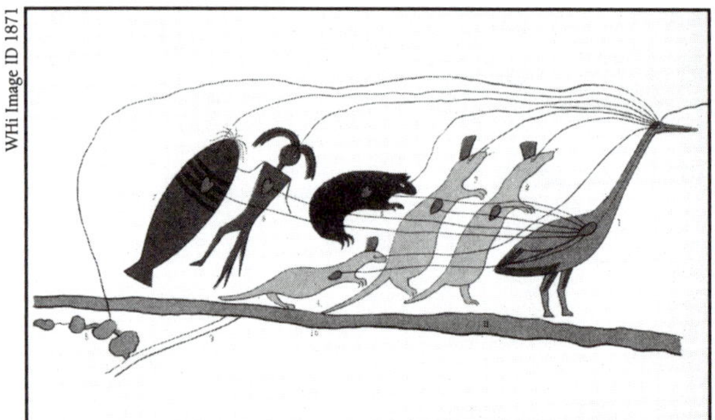

Ojibwe leaders sent this image to Washington, D.C. in 1849. This is how they presented their desires to stay on their land to the government. The lines that link the animals' hearts and eyes flow to a chain of wild rice lakes in the area south of Lake Superior that once was Ojibwe homeland.

Several battles broke out. The Battle of Wisconsin Heights was one. It took place on the high banks of the Wisconsin River, just east of present-day Sauk City. Black Hawk's warriors fought so that other members of the group could cross the river safely. Most of his people escaped alive. But some of Black Hawk's followers died from hunger and weakness as they continued **fleeing** west.

When Black Hawk and his people finally reached the Mississippi, soldiers again ignored the flag of peace. At the mouth of the Bad Axe River, U.S. soldiers fired cannons and rifles at the Indian people who were trying to swim to safety. These soldiers **massacred** (**mass** uh curd) many Indians when they attacked older people, women, and children as well as warriors. Only 150 of Black Hawk's followers survived.

After Black Hawk's surrender, he sadly remembered his old home when "all this land had been ours." He bitterly

    fleeing: Escaping from danger   **massacred:** Fiercely attacked and killed in large numbers

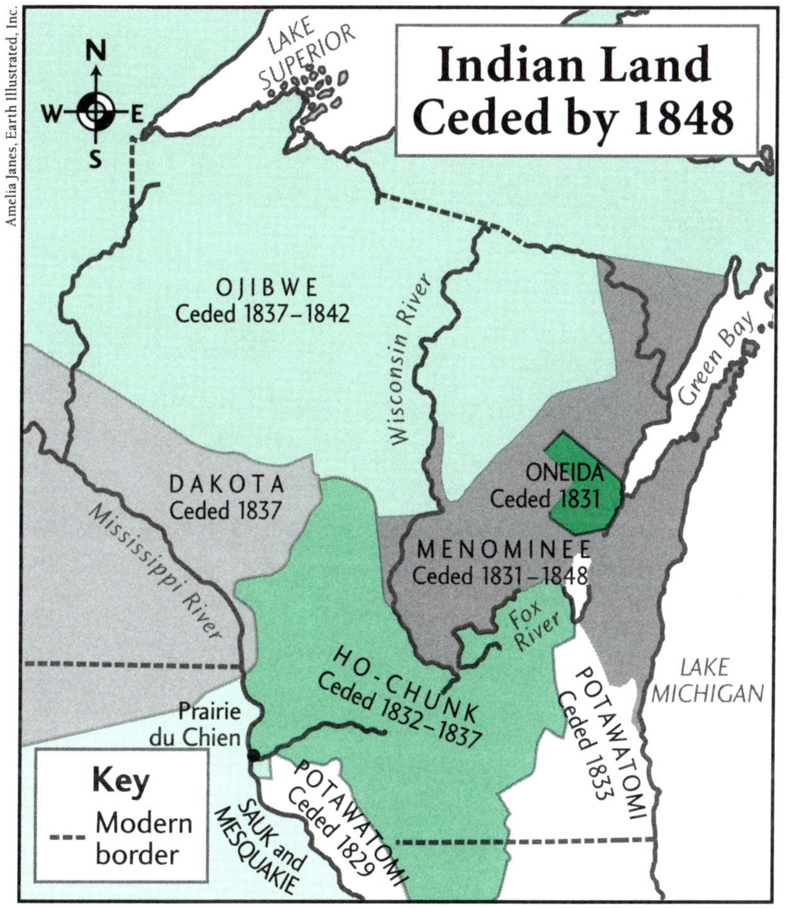

complained that "the whites were not satisfied until they took our village and our graveyards from us, and **removed** us across the Mississippi."

Through treaties negotiated between 1829 and 1833, Indian Nations south and east of the Wisconsin River were forced to **cede** (seed) their lands. After the Black Hawk War, even Indians Nations that had not given Black Hawk any help had to cede land to the government of the United States. Eventually, the U.S. government would sell this land to new settlers.

Although Indians continued to live in Wisconsin, the treaties and laws made it impossible for them to continue their traditional use of the land. New types of land use became common as new settlers moved into the region. After 1836, these newcomers now lived in Wisconsin Territory. In 1848, Wisconsin became a state.

removed: Forced to move   **cede:** Give up

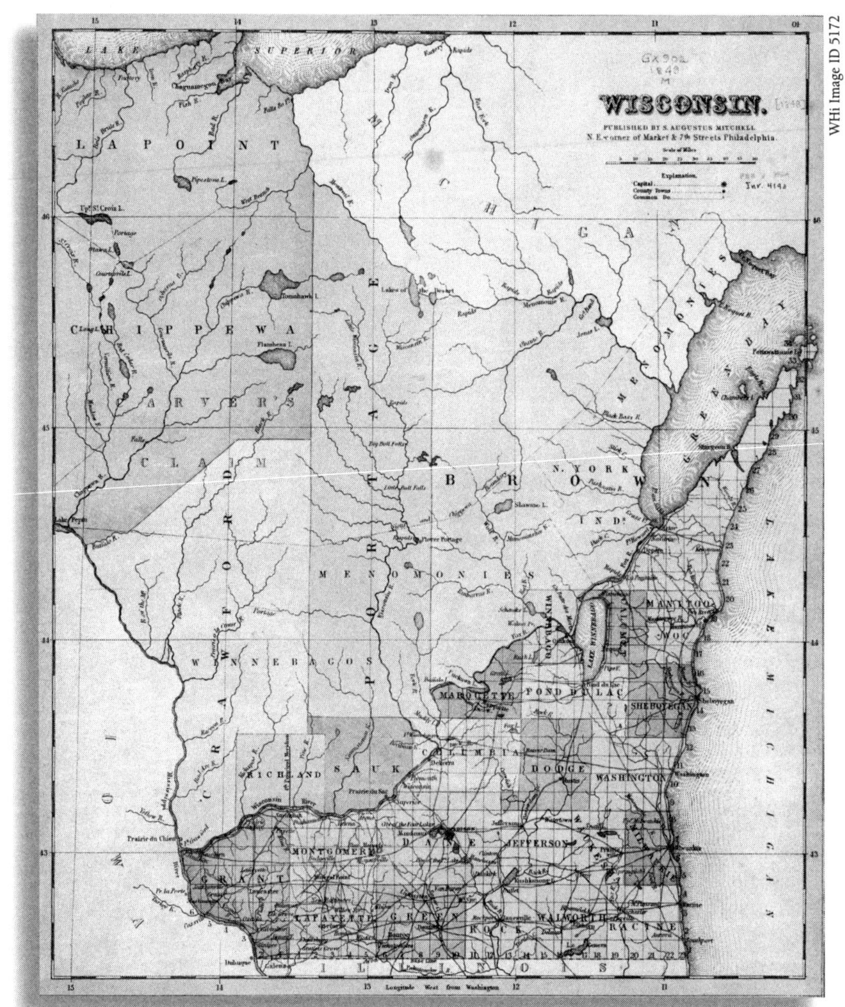

This map of Wisconsin was created in 1848. In what ways is the state different today?

HOW WISCONSIN BECAME A U.S. TERRITORY

Before Wisconsin became the Wisconsin Territory, it was part of 3 other territories. First it was part of the Indiana Territory. Then it was part of the Illinois Territory. Finally, between 1818 and 1836, Wisconsin was part of the Michigan Territory. Wisconsin needed enough non-Indian settlers living in the area to ask the U.S. government to recognize it as a territory of its own. By 1835, enough settlers had arrived.

James Duane Doty was a territorial judge and leader. He worked hard to help Wisconsin become its own territory. Finally, on July 4, 1836, enough non-Indians had moved to the area so that President Andrew Jackson could create the Wisconsin Territory. He appointed one of the American Black Hawk War leaders, General Henry Dodge, as governor. No Native people were a part of the new territorial government. Only non-Indian men were allowed to vote.

WHi Image ID 27177

This drawing from 1834 shows Henry Dodge dressed in frontier clothing.

Chapter 5

Surveying, Selling, and Settling the Land

◆ ◆ ◆

1950 photograph of La Crosse on the Mississippi River. The Mississippi is both a legal and natural boundary between Wisconsin and Minnesota.

If your home covered an entire island, you would have **natural boundaries** separating your family's property from that of anyone else. If not, **legal boundaries** separate your farm, house, or apartment from that of your neighbor. When you look at a map of Wisconsin, you see both natural and legal boundaries. The Mississippi, Montreal, and Menominee rivers form some of Wisconsin's natural boundaries. Lakes Superior and Michigan are 2 huge bodies of water that form Wisconsin's other 2 natural boundaries.

The straight lines along the state's southern border and western border form legal boundaries set by the U.S. government. These legal boundaries separate Wisconsin from Illinois to the south and from Minnesota in the northwest. A **road atlas** shows other divisions: counties, towns, and **townships** that divide areas of land into regular sections. We use boundaries to describe where we live—in a city or town, rural countryside, county, state, or country.

natural boundaries: Features of nature that separate one area from another **legal boundaries:** The lines created by the government that separate one property from another **road atlas:** A book of maps that show roads, boundaries between places, and important landmarks **townships:** Smaller parts of a town that have control over their land

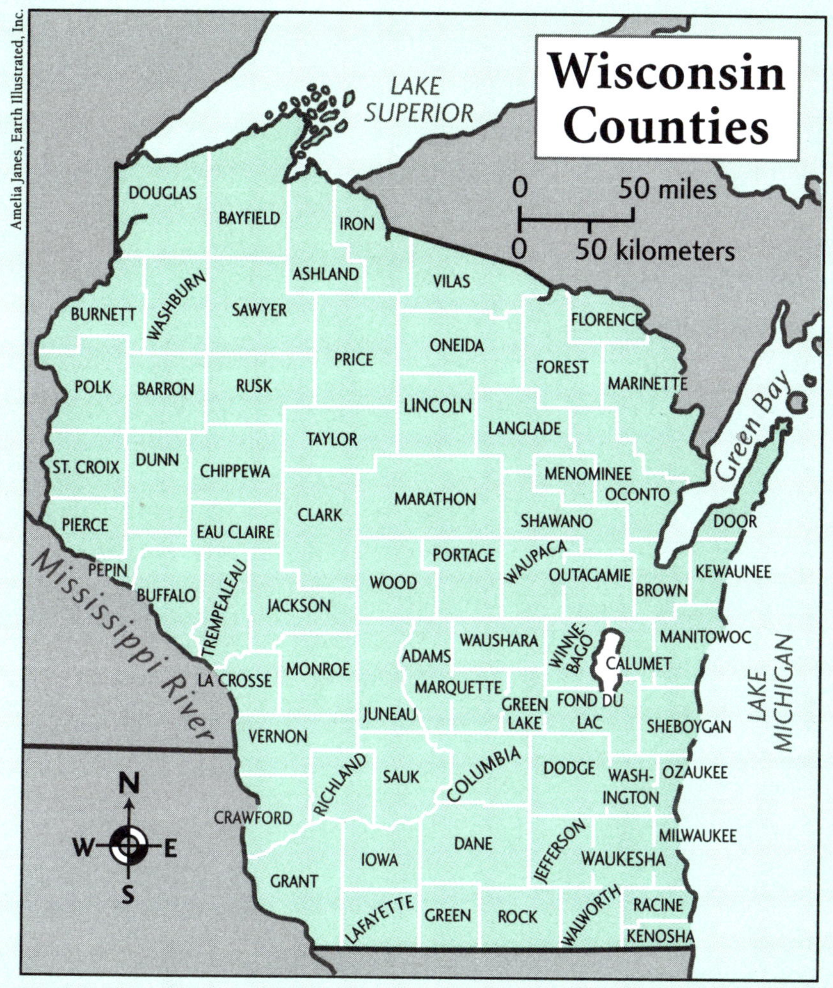

Think About It

Who made decisions about where legal boundaries should be in Wisconsin? How were the legal boundaries measured? How did all of these decisions about dividing land affect the lives of those living in Wisconsin? How do they continue to affect us today?

Laws About Land

The same event often produces very different results for the people involved. For example, Black Hawk's **defeat** in 1832 led to the removal of Indian nations from southern Wisconsin. Being forced to leave their homelands began a tragic chapter in the history of Wisconsin's Indian people.

That same event offered many opportunities for the new non-Indian settlers. For the first time, newcomers from Europe and from the East Coast of America began arriving in large numbers to settle the land and take advantage of its natural resources. These Euro-American settlers brought to Wisconsin their own attitudes and traditions toward land use learned from their European ancestors.

Tribal people held land in common as a *community*. Land was used and shared by all members of their group. But Euro-Americans settled land as *individuals*. They understood land as something that could be bought and sold.

Euro-Americans' use of the land and its resources changed Wisconsin history. We can date this change to the settling of the lead-mining district in the 1820s and to the Black Hawk War that followed.

The Dutch are one group of immigrants who came to Wisconsin. These first settlers built log homes and used horses to travel and to work the land.

 defeat: Loss

Nearly 50 years earlier, the United States was still a very young nation. Our national leaders knew that the country needed land on which to grow. The new **federal government** had passed a special law known as the Land **Ordinance** (**or** duh nuhns) of 1785. The Land Ordinance law became known as the Northwest Ordinance. This law created an orderly way for land that once belonged to Indian tribes to be measured, divided, and sold to settlers moving west.

First the U.S. government received new land through treaties. Then the government **established** a system of dividing and selling land that made it easier to shift control of the land from the government to individual ownership.

Illustration: Jill Bremigan

Surveying the Land

The General Land Office (later called the **Bureau** (**byur** oh) of Land Management) was in charge of the **surveying** (sur **vay** ing) and mapping that began in Wisconsin in 1832, right after Black Hawk's defeat. **Surveyors** used a **rectangular survey** to decide where boundaries should go. This survey allowed a surveyor to divide the land into a rectangular grid (like an imaginary checkerboard) to mark off the land, no matter what the land actually looked like.

The surveyor used imaginary lines

federal government: A type of government where a nation's states are united under and controlled by one government
ordinance: A law or command   **established:** Put in place; started   **bureau:** Office   **surveying:** Exploring and measuring land in order to make a map or plan   **surveyors:** People who determine the geographic appearance or legal boundaries of a place   **rectangular survey:** A system of exploring and measuring land using rectangular shapes to decide where boundaries should be drawn

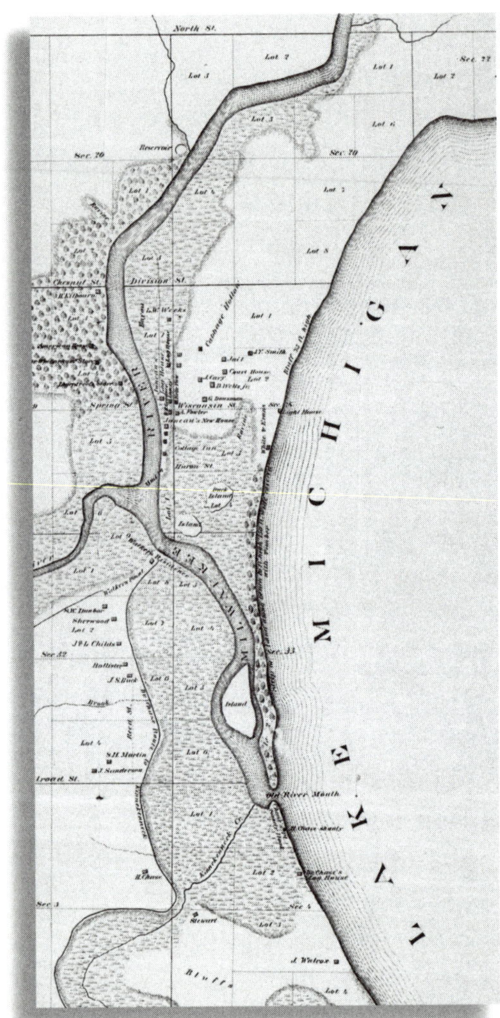

You can see lot lines on this 1876 survey map of Milwaukee.

Surveyors used special equipment—measuring chains, compasses, rods, poles, and marking pins—to measure and mark the land into townships.

running from north to south called **meridians** (mer **rid** ee ans) and imaginary lines running from east to west known as **parallels** to create this grid. These evenly placed lines divided the land into squares—6 miles on each side. Each 6-mile square became a township. Surveyors then divided the township into smaller areas called **lots** to sell to individuals. The rectangular survey worked well because it allowed people to look at maps and see how the land was divided, even if they lived far away at the time.

   meridians: Imaginary lines that run from north to south   **parallels:** Imaginary lines that run from east to west
lots: Pieces of a township that individuals buy

Selling the Land

Surveyors did not create maps themselves. Surveyors kept notebooks full of information and descriptions that **cartographers** (car **tog** gruhf furz) could use to create **plat maps** . Plat maps showed the pieces of property that surveyors had measured, divided, and marked.

People looked at these plat maps to select the property they wanted to buy from the U.S. government. The property cost $1.25 an acre. Surveyors and mapmakers worked quickly. In 1834, the government opened land offices in the 2 areas with the most people: Green Bay and Mineral Point.

cartographers: People who make maps   **plat maps:** Maps of townships showing the boundaries of lots

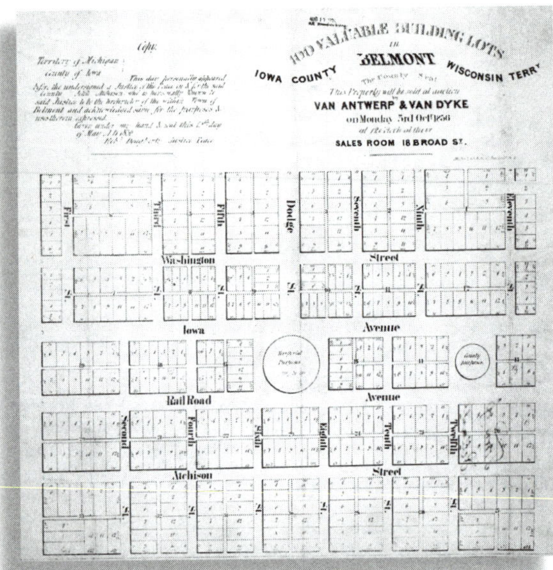
A plat map showing lots that were sold in the town of Belmont in 1836.

Lead miners, farmers, and all kinds of people who wanted to work in growing communities were ready to move to Wisconsin. Some of these settlers worked as carpenters, lawyers, preachers, and storekeepers. They all played a role in developing new communities in Wisconsin. These communities added many new kinds of rural and urban buildings to Wisconsin's built environment.

The government wanted non-Indians to be able to settle easily, so even people without a great deal of money could afford the inexpensive government price.

Still, not all those who wanted land were able to buy it so cheaply. Some people, known as **speculators** (**spek** yuh lay turz), bought land to make money. They held the land until someone offered them money to buy it. Many of the people who bought from speculators wanted to create a farm, construct a store, or build a house. These speculators charged more than $1.25 an acre.

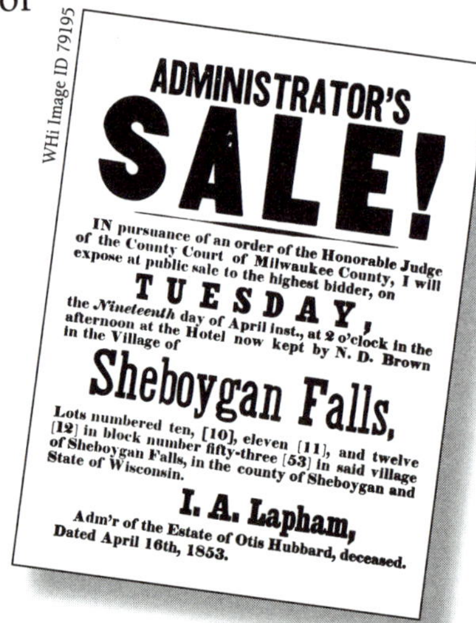

Land sale advertisement from 1853

   speculators: People who invest in something risky in order to make money

Farmers, miners, storekeepers, and speculators expected different things from the land. But all non-Indians believed that land was property. As property it could be bought, sold, and developed. This idea contrasted sharply with the different ways tribal people had used and shared the land's resources before the newcomers arrived. Land ownership created the Wisconsin we know today.

Settling the Land

For thousands of years, waterways had served as the area's **transportation** transportation routes. Wisconsin had a large network of rivers and lakes. The waterways made it easy for canoes to carry tribal people and their belongings from place to place. Later, the Great Lakes carried fur traders from French Canada through Lake Michigan or Lake Superior to Wisconsin. Then Wisconsin's waterways made it easy for canoes to get into the **interior** (in **tir** ee ur) of the state.

The storefronts on East Water Street in Milwaukee, 1844

transportation: Everything having to do with travel   **interior:** An area inside of another

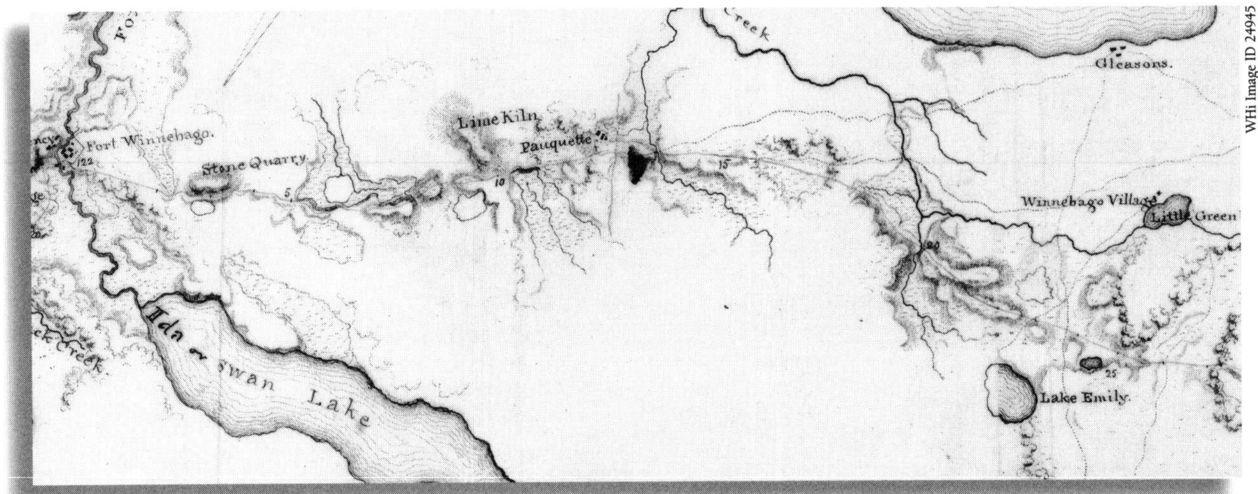

An excellent cartographer, James Duane Doty drew a map of his route from Fort Howard to Fort Crawford in 1833. This is one section of that journey.

This steamboat, the Milwaukie, was used to transport people and goods on the Great Lakes during the early 1800s.

By the early 1800s, steamboats began to carry people and goods on the Great Lakes and on Wisconsin's larger rivers. These large boats could travel faster than canoes and could carry many more people and goods. New settlers began moving to Wisconsin in great numbers in the 1830s. These settlers needed good land routes as well as waterways.

Steamboats could not reach the interior of Wisconsin Territory, and canoes could not easily transport 2 of Wisconsin's important resources: lead and lumber. In the 1830s, lead was the biggest money earner in Wisconsin. Lumber was the key resource used to construct the buildings on new frontier farms and in new frontier communities.

James Duane Doty was a speculator and **developer** in Wisconsin in the 1830s. Doty **proposed** that the U.S. government build a road across the region. The road would connect the U.S. government forts already located along the Fox and Wisconsin rivers. These forts had been built during the fur-trading era at Prairie du Chien, Portage, and Green Bay. The same road that connected the forts would also make it easier to settle, build, and connect the new communities Doty dreamed of building for new settlers.

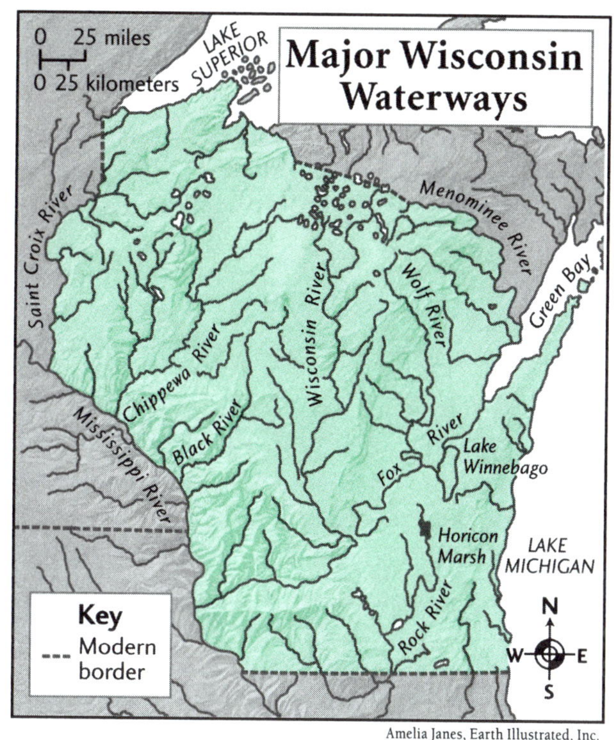

Amelia Janes, Earth Illustrated, Inc.

Doty made several trips on horseback to map the best **route**. For part of the way, his route traced older Indian trails. It also went near rivers and lakes, where settlers could find natural resources and build near the water. The high ground in the southwestern part of the route later became known as the Military Ridge. By 1832,

developer: Someone who transforms land **proposed:** Suggested or offered an idea for discussion
route: A road or course you follow to get from one place to another

The plank road in front of Wade House ran between Sheboygan and Fond du Lac. It was constructed of wooden boards placed on wooden rails. The plank road made horse-drawn tranportation easier and more reliable than dirt roads.

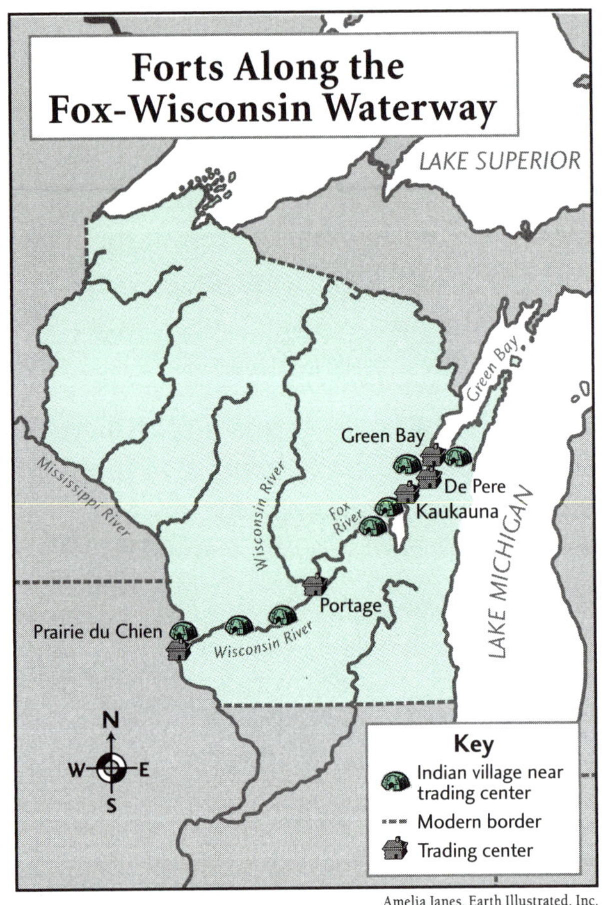

Amelia Janes, Earth Illustrated, Inc.

the government was surveying the area in order to build the road along a route similar to the one that Doty suggested.

The Military Road became Wisconsin's first major land route. The Military Road connected old communities on Lake Michigan and the Mississippi River with the new settlements growing up in the southern part of the state. The road made it easier for settlers to travel with their belongings to their new homes. This road also helped open the interior of Wisconsin to the major new settlements Doty dreamed of.

Land developers like Doty wanted to plan and build entire communities. They hired surveyors and cartographers to map out plans for towns along the Military Road and at other locations near good natural resources. These planned communities became known as "paper towns" because they existed only on paper. The developers hoped that the locations and plans looked inviting enough to attract settlers to the frontier of Wisconsin.

Madison, Wisconsin's capital, began as a paper town. In the winter of 1836, Doty made a trip to the territory's capital at Belmont. There he skillfully **convinced**

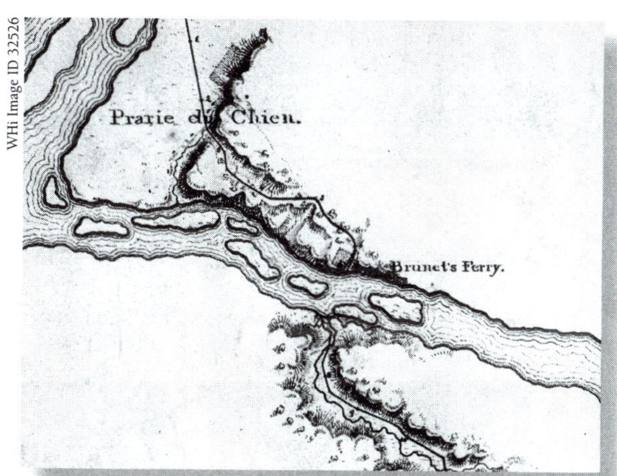

Doty's Military Road (the thin line) crossed the Wisconsin River just below Prairie du Chien.

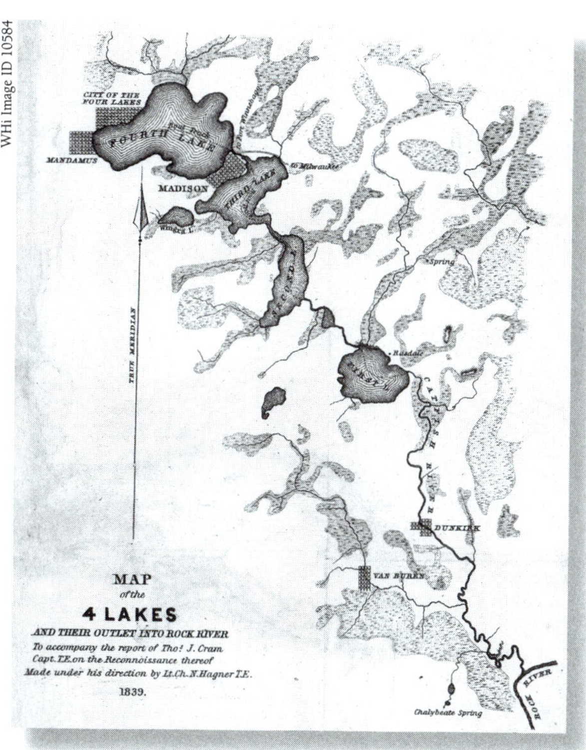

1839 map of the four lakes that surround Madison

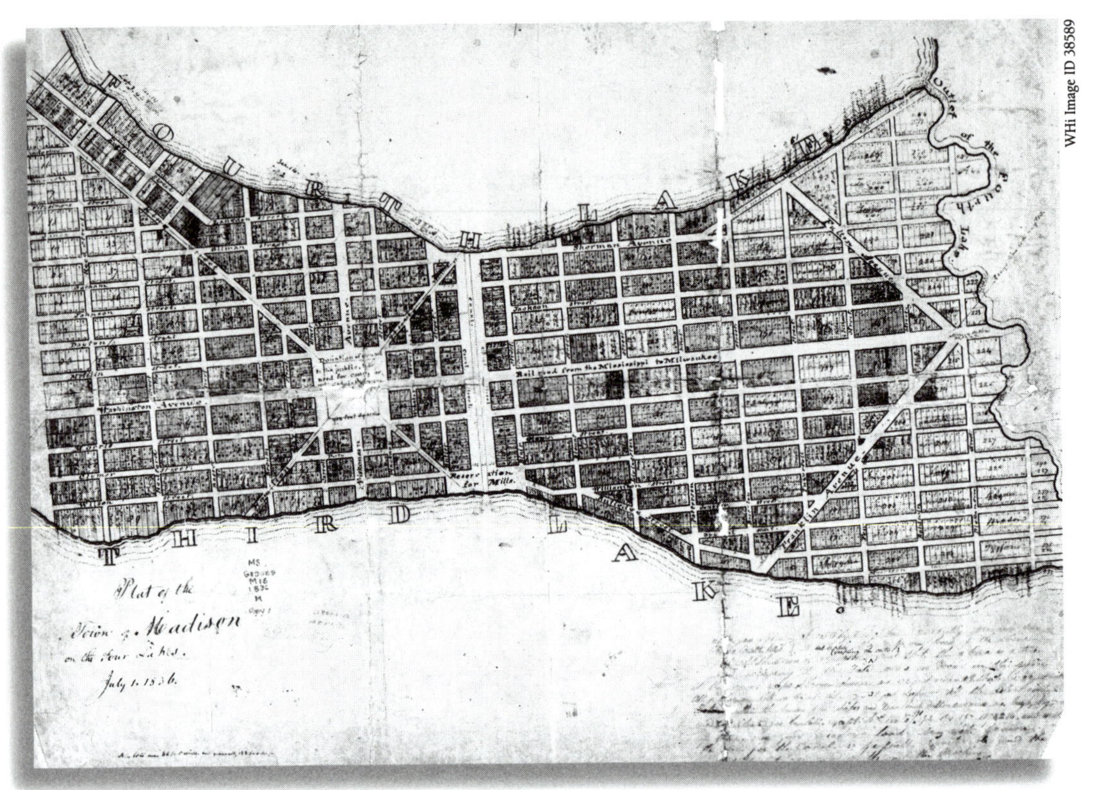

This 1836 plat map of Madison shows the **isthmus** (**is** muhs), the narrow strip of land between the "Fourth Lake" and the "Third Lake."

the territorial **legislators** (**lej** uh slay turz) that the Four Lakes area in south central Wisconsin would make a perfect location for a state capital.

Belmont was in the southwestern part of the state—far from both Green Bay and Milwaukee, where most people in territorial Wisconsin lived. The Four Lakes area was in the south-central part of Wisconsin, halfway between Lake Michigan and the

   isthmus: A narrow strip of land between two bodies of water   **legislators:** People who make laws

Mississippi River, and not far from the Military Road. Doty explained that the Four Lakes area would be easier to reach from Green Bay or Milwaukee. He had already drawn plans for Madison, the paper town he hoped would become the capital.

The legislators agreed to move the capital to the Four Lakes area, even though Ho-Chunk villagers and a few fur-trading households were the only people already living there. No settlers lived in the Madison area at the time. Some paper towns like Madison, Neenah, Menasha, and Fond du Lac (**fahn** duh lak) were also developed by Doty. These towns succeeded. But others never grew as land developers hoped.

The first house to be built in Madison was the Peck Cabin.

New non-Indian ideas about land use were permanently changing Wisconsin's landscape. These ideas had already shaped older communities such as Green Bay and Prairie du Chien. Now non-Indian villages, towns, and even the rural land around them began to form the human-shaped environment that dominates Wisconsin's landscape today.

Chapter 6

Timber!

◆ ◆ ◆

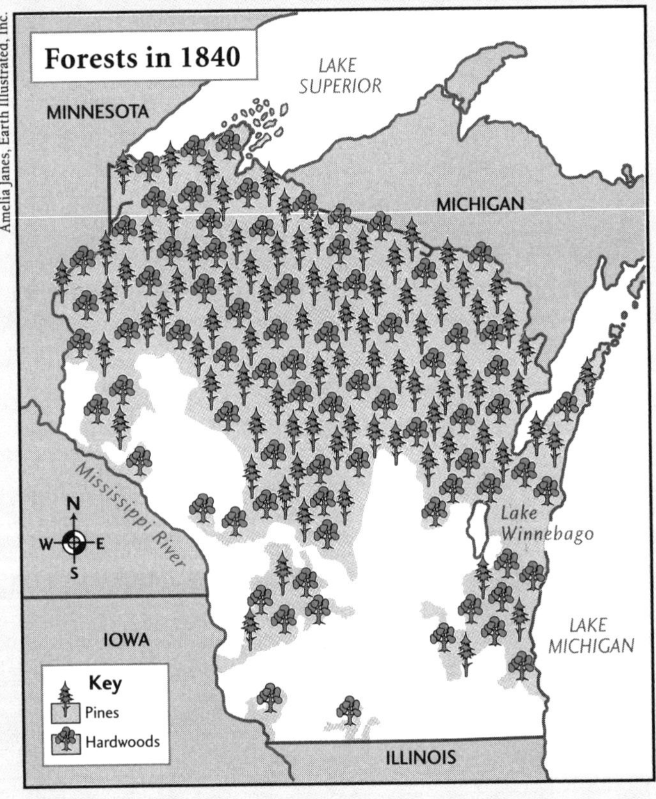

Look at the large map on this page. It shows the kind of trees that covered Wisconsin when it became a state in 1848. At that time, forests took up about three-fourths of the state. **Lumbermen** realized that these forests could support a huge **lumber industry** .

One Wisconsin politician bragged that the forests could supply "all the wants of all **citizens** (**sit** uh zuhns) for all time to come." Just as he hoped, the **lumber** from Wisconsin's forests helped build farms and homes and other buildings for settlers. Then settlers from the East moved farther west, to places like Nebraska and

70   **lumbermen:** Forest and sawmill owners   **lumber industry:** The business of logging trees and turning them into boards and planks that can be sold to construct homes and other buildings   **citizens:** Members of a particular community who have certain rights   **lumber:** Boards sawed from logs at a sawmill

the Dakota Territory. They lived in places where wood was not available. It had to be shipped from places that had more trees. Wood from Wisconsin's forests was shipped first by waterways as far as Chicago, St. Louis, and even New Orleans. Later, in the late 1870s, railroads began to deliver Wisconsin logs. By 1889, Wisconsin was the biggest producer of lumber in America!

A large group gathers to help build a barn in Hillsboro in 1885

Those Wisconsin pine forests that seemed able to supply "all the wants of all citizens for all time to come" had nearly disappeared by 1900. It took many years to renew and restore this important natural resource.

Think About It

Why have forests been so important to people in Wisconsin? How has their use changed over time? Why did so many forests disappear in such a short time? How did land use in northern Wisconsin change as a result? How do people manage our forests today so that they will last and be **sustainable** (suh **stayn** uh buhl)?

sustainable: Using a resource so that it can be used today and in the future

71

Native People and Wisconsin Forests

When Wisconsin was settled, most of Wisconsin's forests were in the northern two-thirds of the state, the homeland of the Ojibwe and Menominee tribes. Native people in northern Wisconsin relied on many resources of the forest. They relied on animals for food, clothing, and shelter. They gathered forest plants for food and medicine. They used the trees to build birch-bark canoes and wigwams made of saplings and bark. They also used the wood to heat their homes and to cook food.

In the 1830s, settlers from the East started to make their home in northern Wisconsin. Just as it had in the southern part of the state, the U.S. government wanted the Indian nations in the north to give up their land for the new settlers. The settlers hoped to use the forest to build homes, to sell wood, and to clear the land for farms. The U.S. government put pressure on the northern Indian nations. Eventually, it forced them to sign treaties to give up much of their tribal lands.

Our Forests Build a New State and Nation

The forested areas of the Upper Midwest have always shaped the lives of those who lived in the region. Early pioneers used the trees around them to make tools and to build homes, barns, early wooden "plank" roads, businesses, churches, and schools. They also needed large amounts of wood for cooking and heating.

The forests of Wisconsin held many kinds of trees. Some were **hardwoods**. Others were **softwoods**. The white pine was the mightiest of all Great Lakes trees. It grew in great numbers in the northern part of Wisconsin.

  hardwoods: Broad-leafed trees that lose their leaves, such as birch, maple, and oak   **softwoods:** Cone-bearing evergreens such as pine, spruce, and hemlock

White pine was the tree cut down by early **lumberjacks**. These trees could be 2 to 6 feet wide and 6 to 18 feet around. Those that became **mature** (muh **chur**) grew to be 100 feet tall. Some lived for 250 years or more. Four of these giant trees were enough to build an entire house. So much white pine existed in northern Wisconsin that the area became known as the "pinery."

White pine was not only the largest of the trees in northern Wisconsin. It was a softwood, and could also float. Floating logs downstream was the only way that lumberjacks could move these huge logs to **sawmills**. At the sawmill, logs would be turned into lumber, ready to be used in making wood products such as furniture, barrels, fence posts, shingles, and houses.

These lumberjacks used a two-person saw to cut a downed tree into smaller pieces.

Lumberjacks hauling logs with the help of oxen teams during the winter of 1880

lumberjacks: People who worked in the woods and lived in the lumber camps   **mature:** Full-grown   **sawmills:** Places where workers use machines to cut logs into lumber

As the lumber industry grew in the 1850s and 1860s, northern Wisconsin's river systems became busy water highways for shipping lumber to faraway cities. The biggest lumber districts in the state took their names from the rivers where they were located: Wisconsin, Menominee, Wolf, Black, St. Croix, and Chippewa. Towns such as Oshkosh, Wausau, Stevens Point, Chippewa Falls, La Crosse, and Eau Claire grew along with the lumber industry on the banks of these waterways. Sawmills supplied lumber for Wisconsin and for the nation.

The lumber industry in Northern Wisconsin began with cutting the **prized** white pine. Lumberjacks in the early logging camps cut only the largest, most mature trees. They cut down the trees in the wintertime. During the winter lumberjacks made iced roads in the snow. Oxen or horses hauled the logs to loading

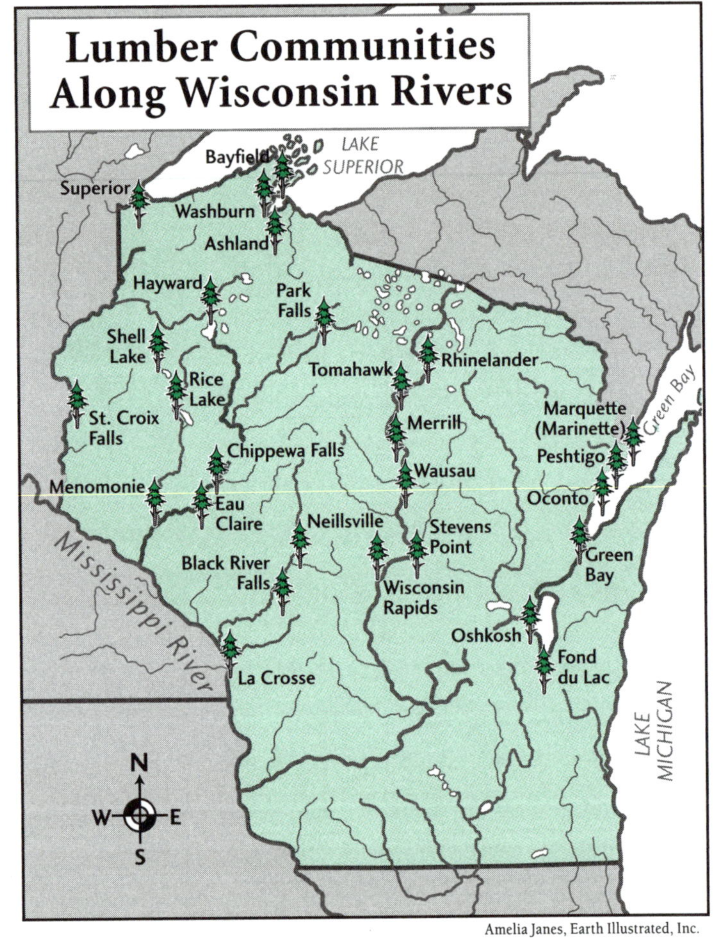

Amelia Janes, Earth Illustrated, Inc.

     prized: Seen as valuable

areas on the riverbanks. In the spring the snow melted and raised the level of the water in the streams and rivers. With the rivers full of water, the lumberjacks floated the logs downriver to the sawmills during a **log drive** . After the log drive, some of the men returned home to be with their families and farm until the next winter.

The sawmill in Emerson, 1908

Logs piled high on a sleigh during the winter logging season

log drive: An event each spring when logs were floated down the river in great numbers

WHAT WAS WORK LIKE IN A LOGGING CAMP?

Logging camps were busy from before the sun went up to sundown. Below are many of the jobs that required strong workers with special skills:

The **foreman** had the most responsibilities. He went out in the early fall to look over the woods and select the site for the logging camp. Then he and a crew of men built the camp buildings. The foreman was in charge of day-to-day business.

The **cook** was second only to the foreman in importance. The cook and his helper, the **cookee** (**ku** kee), made all the meals that hungry, hardworking men needed to do their work. Sometimes women worked as cook or cookee.

The **saw filer** was the next most important man in camp. The filer sharpened the saws the men used to cut down trees and to cut trees into logs. Without sharp saws no work would get done.

The men of Rice Lake Lumbering Camp #6, in Barron County, washing their clothes during the winter of 1913. Sunday was always wash day.

Men did the cooking at the lumber camp. Here are the cook and cookee at a camp in Hayward.

A log driving crew breaks up a log jam near Chippewa Falls.

The **blacksmith** made tools such as axes, gear for the horses and oxen, and kitchen equipment to help feed the hungry workers. Most things made of iron or tin were made and repaired by the blacksmith.

A **greenhorn** was a new lumberjack who didn't have much experience.

In the early days of logging **choppers** used axes to chop down trees. Later, **fellers** used long **crosscut saws** to saw a tree down.

Skidders were in charge of dragging logs to the **skidways** . **Swampers** cut brush and kept roads repaired for the skidders. They also cut the branches that were not needed for making lumber off the tree trunks.

Teamsters drove teams of oxen or horses that pulled sleighs loaded with logs down to the river.

The **scaler** measured each log to figure out how much wood was in it.

The **river pig** followed the logs down the river to the sawmill, sometimes walking along the banks of the river and other times hopping from log to log.

The Lumber Industry: Risk, Growth, and New Technology

Starting in the 1850s, the need for Wisconsin's lumber grew rapidly. There were many newcomers to Wisconsin during these years: both American-born and immigrants. More lumber was needed to supply fast-growing towns and cities across Wisconsin and the nation.

At the same time, people were moving beyond the Great Lakes to settle on the Great Plains. The Great Plains offered plenty of rich prairie land for farming but few forests. The **demand** for lumber was great.

For the **entrepreneurs** (ahn truh pruh **nurz**) who started logging companies, this was a great opportunity. If they could get lumber to the areas that needed it, they could make a profit. But it was also a period of great risk. Entrepreneurs needed large amounts of money to hire men, feed them all winter, buy and feed the horses or oxen, and buy equipment. Men like Henry Stout and Isaac Stephenson are remembered today as great entrepreneurs of Wisconsin's logging industry. There were also loggers who were not successful entrepreneurs. Eugene Shepard lost about as much money as he made, but he became famous for his Paul Bunyan stories.

Do you know any Paul Bunyan tall tales?

   demand: Need   **entrepreneurs:** People who start their own business from scratch

Early logging companies were helped by 2 things. First, they were helped by the great number of immigrants moving to Wisconsin who were willing to work in the northern forests. Second, they were helped by new technologies that allowed lumberjacks to cut more logs in the same amount of time.

When lumberjacks first began logging in northern Wisconsin, they only used axes to cut down the best and oldest pines. But in the 1880s, a major improvement arrived: the crosscut saw, with **raker teeth** that cut wood more quickly. This new technology allowed workers to cut 2 to 3 times as many trees each day!

Railroad tracks reached northern Wisconsin in the 1870s and 1880s. Railroads weren't a new technology. But it had taken nearly 30 years for their tracks to reach the northwoods. Railroads changed the entire logging industry. Lumber companies could now ship logs by train to the sawmill.

With the arrival of the railroads, lumberjacks could now cut down hardwoods, which do not float. Any type of

By 1882, there were railroads across the state. Why do you think there are more railroads in the south than in the north?

raker teeth: Teeth in a crosscut saw that get rid of excess sawdust as they cut through the wood, making cutting faster

wood could be shipped by rail. All of these changes made the lumber business grow even more rapidly. By the mid-1880s, more people worked in lumber-related jobs than in any other industry in the state.

The Forests: Logged and Burned

Men building the railroad in Marathon County in 1890. Both oxen and horses were used for this hard work.

The natural environment of northern Wisconsin began to undergo major changes as a result of logging. When lumberjacks first began logging the forests of northern Wisconsin, they were mostly interested in white pine. They cut the largest trees as quickly as they could. They left behind branches and other **slash** . Sometimes sparks from a train or lightning caused the slash to catch fire. Railroad workers and farmers also used fire to clear all the slash in their way. These fires could get out of control and destroy huge forested areas.

Many people worked both in the forests and in the towns producing lots of lumber. But people paid little attention to what was happening to their environment. Early sawmills created lots of lumber, shingles, and doors. But they also created a great deal of waste. Oshkosh was known as "Sawdust City" because of its many sawmills on the low and marshy banks of the Fox River. So much sawdust and slash stacked up that people used it to raise the level of the land. Today, entire blocks of the city are built on top of sawdust!

80   **slash:** Branches, leaves, and twigs left after cutting a tree

Sawmills in Oshkosh
CONGRESS AVE.
W. NEW YORK AVE.
JACKSON ST.
N. MAIN ST.
ALGOMA BLVD.
HIGH AVE.
Fox River
PEARL ST.
WITZEL AVE.
BROAD ST.
BAY ST.
MILL ST.
W. 9TH AVE.
OHIO ST.
OREGON ST.
Lake Winnebago
N
W   E
S
Key
Sawmill
Railroad
Oshkosh
Amelia Janes, Earth Illustrated, Inc.

Parts of the Oconto, Peshtigo (**pesh** ti goh), and Menominee rivers near the towns with sawmills became clogged with sawdust, small branches, and slash. These and other rivers like them had to be **dredged** so that large boats could travel through. Clogging of streams and rivers was a problem. But the danger of forest fires was even more frightening. On October 8, 1871, the worst of these disasters occurred—the Great Peshtigo Fire. The weather had been unusually dry that summer and autumn. And the cleared forests were filled with stumps and dry slash.

Terrific storm winds blew in from the west. Small fires combined with the winds to form a flaming **firestorm** . The fire headed toward Peshtigo. There it destroyed nearly everything in its path—sawmills, churches, homes, hotels, and businesses. The fire also killed almost half of the 1,700 people who lived or worked in Peshtigo. More people were killed in other communities in the path of the fire. Reverend Peter Pernin of Peshtigo survived by jumping into the river. Later he wrote that looking up from the water, "I saw nothing but flames; houses, trees, and the air itself were on fire."

   dredged: Dug or scooped out   **firestorm:** A fire of great size and heat that is fed by strong winds

The fire was so strong it crossed the waters of Green Bay. Flames even took the community of Williamsville in Door County. Today, a historical marker is all that is left of the village, which burned to the ground the day of the Great Peshtigo Fire. The Peshtigo Fire was the largest fire in Wisconsin history, burning nearly 2500 square miles of land. Loss from destructive forest fires continued to be a problem for the people in northern Wisconsin.

Illustration of the Peshtigo river on fire from Harper's Weekly, *November 25, 1871.*

◆ ◆ ◆

The forests that people in 1860 thought were endless were almost gone in less than 50 years. Only 8 million of the 17 million trees in Wisconsin in 1850 were still standing in 1898. Left behind was a landscape without the great forests that the early explorers knew.

Most Americans then believed that all land could and should be "improved" to make it useful. They felt that forests existed mainly to supply wood for wood

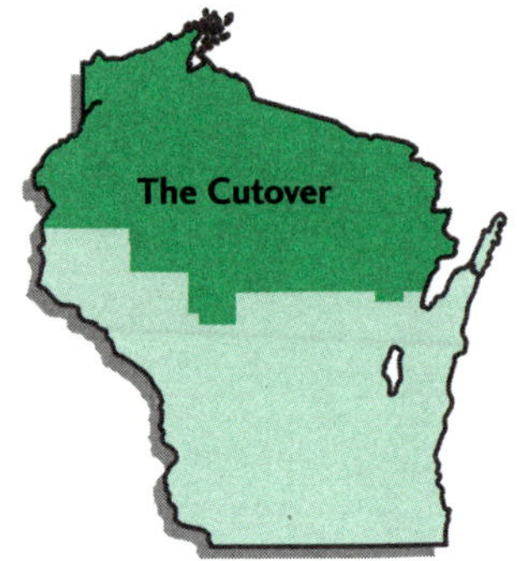

This booklet was written in Polish to convince immigrants to buy farmland in Wisconsin.

products. Once the forests were gone, many people believed that the same land could be farmed. By the late 1890s, only stumps remained over much of northern Wisconsin. Some lumber communities became deserted ghost towns after the trees disappeared. This region became known as "the **Cutover** ."

Many people thought that farmers looking for cheap land could remove the stumps and begin to raise crops. William Henry, **dean** of the College of Agriculture at the University of Wisconsin, created a small book "to draw to Wisconsin a **desirable** (di **zı** ruh buhl) class of farmers." *Northern Wisconsin: A Handbook for the Homeseeker* contained photos of farmers in the Cutover with their healthy harvests from the 1895 growing season. The *Handbook for the Homeseeker*

Men clearing stumps in Medford with the help of a stump-clearing machine, 1895.

    Cutover: The vast stretch of land in northern Wisconsin that was heavily logged, leaving a cleared landscape **dean:** Head **desirable:** Worth having

was printed in English, German, and Norwegian and sent to countries in northern Europe. These booklets told Europeans about available cheap land in the Cutover and promised immigrant farmers good land at cheap prices. It even promised crops that never failed.

The booklets made promises that couldn't be kept. Many immigrants came and worked hard to clear the stumps and to establish farms. Over 20,000 new farms were started between 1880 and 1900! But as Chapter 1 shows us, soil that is good for growing trees is not always good for growing crops. Also, the growing season in northern Wisconsin is very short. Many farms failed in the Cutover—no matter how hard the farmers worked. By 1900, many of these farms were abandoned and over 10,000 families had failed at farming.

Champions of the Forest

The Peshtigo Fire shocked and saddened people. But few people were concerned about the great changes that the fire and **overlogging** brought to northern Wisconsin. Scientist Increase Lapham was one of those who cared about these changes. Four years before the Peshtigo Fire, in 1867, he prepared a report on "The Destruction of Forest Trees Now Going on So Rapidly in Wisconsin." He argued that it should be the duty of the state "to perfect our knowledge of the growth and proper management of forest trees." It would take 40 years—just after 1900—before people realized how much of the forest was gone and that they needed to do something about it.

Increase Lapham

overlogging: Logging all of the trees in one area so that none are left to reproduce

Chief Oshkosh

People realized that forests *were* the crop of the northern part of the state only *after* farming in the Cutover failed. Just as Increase Lapham had suggested, forests could be kept healthy if lumberjacks cut down *only* those trees that were old enough—greater than 70 years old. In some areas new trees grew from seeds on their own, but people in the Cutover needed to plant new trees.

Lapham's ideas for **forest management** were in line with what the Menominee nation had been doing since at least the 1830s. The Menominee believe in taking only what they need from their "grandmother," Mother Earth, or ***Kohkomaehsaehkomikanaeh*** (koh koh ma saw koh **mee** ka nuh). Tribal elders at that time were already passing on a tradition of sustainable forest management, although they may not have thought of it in those terms. Menominee leader Chief Oshkosh said, "Start at one end of the reservation and cut the mature trees, and by the time you reach the other end of the reservation, it will be time to start over again." From 1908 to 1910, the Menominee and the U.S. Department of Agriculture worked together on **selective cutting** of mature trees on tribal land.

In 1904, Edward Merriam Griffith became Wisconsin's first **state forester**. He was hired just after Wisconsin had logged more trees than any other state in the nation. From 1902 to 1904, Wisconsin was again the number one producer of lumber. Griffith and his staff worked to restore and take care of the forests. They created programs to control fires and insects and helped gain more land for state **forest preserves**.

---

forest management: Using techniques to conserve and promote forests   **selective cutting:** Cutting down mature trees so that younger trees may grow   **state forester:** Person hired by the state to care for its forest   **forest preserves:** Forest land managed by the state

Griffith also helped bring the Forest Products Laboratory to Madison in 1910. In this laboratory, scientists tackled problems such as how to get the very most from trees that are harvested. They studied the types of trees that could be used to make houses, boats, and other wood products while keeping forests healthy.

Scientists have come up with better ways to construct the homes we live in and have created new ways to make paper from trees. In 1911, Griffith started the first state tree **nursery** at Trout Lake in Vilas County. Two years later, the very first Trout Lake tree **seedlings** were planted at Star Lake to start the state's first tree **plantation** . Griffith hoped that Star Lake could be used to teach others about the value of forested lands.

When Griffith left his job in 1915, **reforestation** (ree for uh **stay** shuhn) temporarily came to a halt. It wasn't until the late 1920s that more people realized the importance of Griffith's work. By this time, many farms in the Cutover had been abandoned. No one paid taxes on the land of these failed farms, so the land now belonged to the counties. What could be done with all of this unused land?

Planting trees at Trout Lake's tree nursery in 1916

The state's first tree nursery was at Trout Lake.

nursery: A place where trees and plants are grown from seedlings to be planted on state and private lands **seedlings:** Young plants grown from a seed **plantation:** A large farm **reforestation:** Planting trees to replace those that have been logged or destroyed by disease or fire

Rebuilding and Sustainably Caring for Our Forests

Officials in Oneida County had been against Griffith's ideas in 1913, but 10 years later, the county was the leader in promoting **county forests**. Today, 17 counties in northern Wisconsin own more public forest land than is in Wisconsin's state and national forests. In the late 1920s, the state passed a law that helped private landowners reforest the land. People could afford to improve their land by helping it return to crops of trees rather than farm crops.

In 1928, the Laona School District in Forest County established the first **school forests** in America. There, students learned about tree planting, tree thinning, fire control, and woodland management. The Nicolet and Chequamegon (shuh **wah** muh guhn) **National Forests** were established in 1933. Much of it was land that used to be part of the Cutover.

In the 1920s, some paper companies and lumber companies changed the way they used the forests. Paper companies like Consolidated Water Power and Paper and the Nekoosa-Edwards Paper Company planted **industrial forests**. These forests were allowed to grow much like Griffith's tree plantation at Star Lake. Once trees were 30 years old, they could be harvested and turned into pulp for making paper. Then the trees were replanted like a crop, such as corn.

Illustration: Jill Bremigan

county forests: Forests owned and taken care of by state counties   **school forests:** Forests owned by school districts to teach students about forest management   **national forests:** Forests owned and taken care of by the United States
industrial forests: Forests owned and taken care of by industry

Lumber companies in the 1920s began selective logging and reforestation. In 1926, the Goodman Lumber Company started selective logging of hardwoods. Only trees that were mature were cut for lumber. The next year, they started a tree plantation. In 1927, other companies such as the Connor Lumber and Land Company also started reforestation, and in 1928 they began selective logging. Selective logging gives young trees more room to grow.

The efforts of these companies encouraged other lumber and paper companies to take care of forests sustainably. Today, lumber companies no longer need to plant new trees, because they continue to practice selective logging and **sustainable yield forestry** . Paper companies still plant and harvest their own industrial forests.

In 1929 the **Great Depression** struck the United States. Many people throughout the country were out of work. In 1933, the federal government began the Civilian Conservation Corps (CCC) to help put men back to work. In Wisconsin, CCC workers built state parks, helped control forest fires, and worked on many other projects that helped Wisconsin take better care of its forests. They also planted over 200 million tree seedlings! When the United States entered **World War II** in 1941, the CCC came to an end. But there were others in Wisconsin ready to continue restoring the forest.

In 1944, 9 paper mills and electric companies along the Wisconsin River organized Trees for Tomorrow. This organization taught many people about **land stewardship** in order to make their lands produce young forests. Today, Trees for Tomorrow is still working to help educate teachers, students, and the public about how to take care of Wisconsin forests.

sustainable yield forestry: Harvesting fewer trees than the forest produces naturally **Great Depression:** The years following the 1929 stock market crash when many people were without jobs **World War II:** A war fought in Europe and Asia from 1939 to 1945 **land stewardship:** Taking responsibility to care for the land so that resources will be available in the future

Many more organizations have helped spread the message of land stewardship. Project Learning Tree, a part of the American Forest Foundation, helps support **environmental education** in schools in America and around the world. Camp 5 Wisconsin Forestry Museum in Laona is a museum that used to be a logging camp.

This 1939 poster encouraged young men to join the CCC.

Other logging museums you can visit include the Menominee Logging Museum on the Menominee Reservation in Keshena, the Rhinelander Logging Museum, and the Paul Bunyan Logging Camp Museum in Eau Claire.

Today, thanks to the efforts of forest stewards like these, much of northern Wisconsin's forested land has been restored. Now Wisconsin has more than 16 million acres of forest! Today's forests have many kinds of softwoods and hardwoods.

About 1 in 6 people in Wisconsin has a job related to forestry. Some are foresters or park rangers, some teach forestry to others, and some work in a nursery, paper or lumber mill, or lumber yard—just to name a few. The forest products industry is one of the largest in the state.

Over 70 percent of forest land belongs to private owners, which include individuals and industries. Almost one-third of forest land belongs to county, state, urban, and

    environmental education: Teaching about how to care for the environment

national forests—at places like Brule River State Forest and the Chequamegon-Nicolet (shuh **wah** muh gen   ni koh **lay**) National Forest. The trees you see in cities are part of what's called the **urban forest** . Trees add beauty to city streets, clean the air, and block noise.

There are more than 2.4 billion trees in Wisconsin! Today, the biggest threats to the forest come from tree diseases, insects, fire, and people who don't know about forest management. Forests will last forever if we use sustainable practices. Learning how our forests grow is something we can all take part in. By planting trees, visiting and enjoying different forests, and volunteering, we act as **stewards** of Wisconsin's forests so that they will last forever.

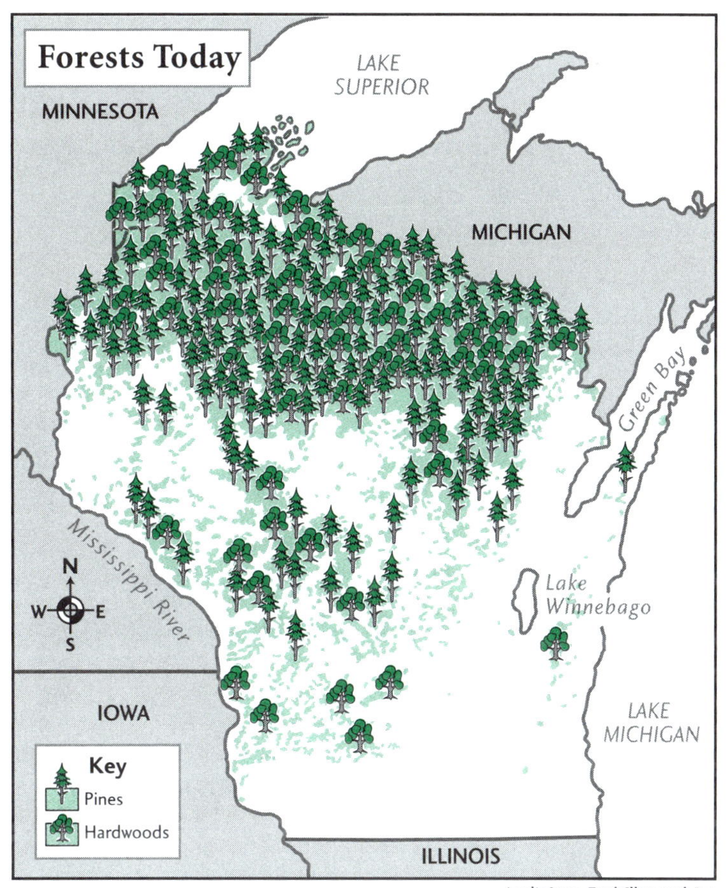

Amelia Janes, Earth Illustrated, Inc.

Chapter 7

From Wheat to Milk and More

◆ ◆ ◆

Children playing in a pool in Milwaukee.

When you grow up in Wisconsin, you learn to wear a warm jacket when it gets cold. And when it gets hot, you can go out in a T-shirt and shorts. You don't take out your sled or hockey stick in July or your roller blades in January. In other words, people match their clothes and their choice of **recreation** (rek ree **ay** shuhn) to the weather.

Successful farmers who make a living from the land know that they need to pay attention to the weather, to seasons, and to the needs of their land. Farmers know that

92   **recreation:** The sports or hobbies that people enjoy in their spare time

the kinds of animals
they raise or the
kinds of crops they
grow have to work
well with the soil,
the rainfall, and the
seasons. Wisconsin
farmers think about
the particular needs
of their land. They
make decisions
based on their
understanding of
the land's ability
to **produce** .

The Stephenson family shows the harvest from their family farm in Marinette in 1895.
What types of vegetables did they grow?

Farmers work hard trying to figure out the best crops for their land. They also have to experiment to find new ways to keep the land fertile.

Think About It

How do those who work the land make their choices? How has farming changed over the past 200 years? How have these changes affected the land? How do the decisions that farmers make affect the rest of us?

produce: To make

Looking Back

Before Europeans entered Wisconsin, the Indians living here had developed their own patterns of land use that worked with the environment. Later, these native people supplied European explorers and fur traders with food. Indians also introduced Europeans to Wisconsin's native foods, like cranberries, corn, and wild rice. For hundreds of years they had also been raising corn, beans, squash, and pumpkins.

Ho-Chunk picking cranberries on Gebhardt's Marsh, Black River Falls, 1913.

Starting in the 1820s and 1830s, non-Indian families came to Wisconsin because they wanted to farm, and in particular to farm wheat. Wisconsin had plenty of cheap and excellent farmland, especially in the fertile southern half of the state. Many pioneers came to Wisconsin from the eastern United States or Europe. They bought land for as little as $1.25 an acre. This land was very fertile because it had been covered with **prairie sod** for hundreds of years.

94   **prairie:** A large area of flat or rolling grassland with few or no trees   **sod:** The top layer of grass and soil

These farmers brought their own farming traditions with them. They discovered that they had to **adapt** these traditions to the particular area where they settled. The newcomers had much to learn.

Wisconsin as a Breadbasket

By 1836, enough people had settled here to form the Wisconsin Territory. By 1848, enough settlers had arrived to become a state. Most pioneer farmers settled in a wide belt of land that stretched from the southeast along Lake Michigan to the northwest along the Mississippi River. These farm families needed wheat to bake their daily bread. They were familiar with growing wheat and planted it as their main crop. They expected it to grow well in the fertile prairie soil. Growing wheat did not require much time or expensive equipment. Wheat also did not need constant care once it was planted.

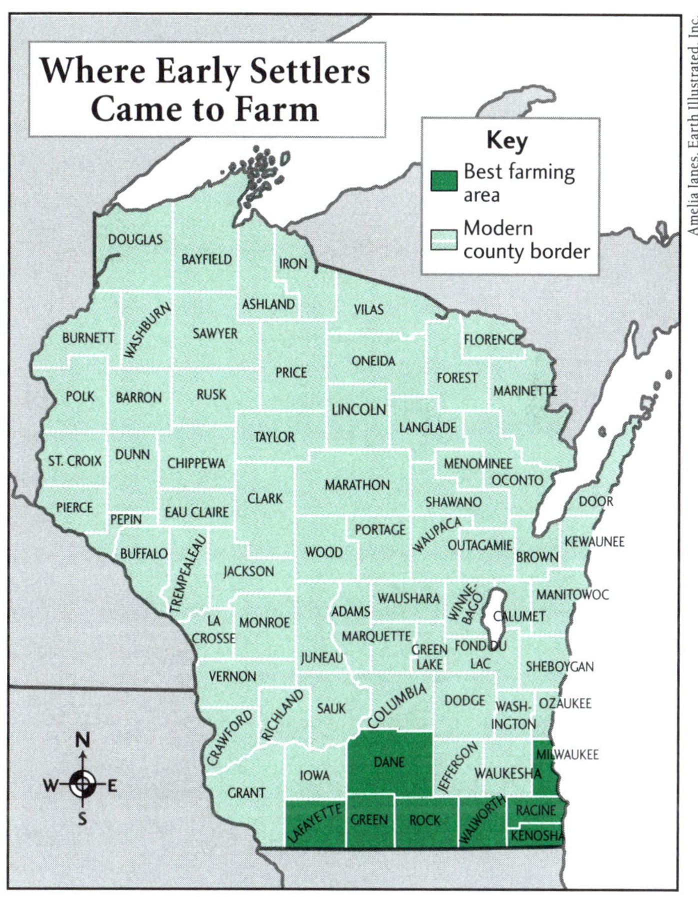

Wisconsin's most desirable farmland was in the southern part of the state.

Mechanized (**mek** uh nızd) equipment made farmers' work easier. Midwest inventors such as Cyrus (**SI** ris) McCormick of the Shenandoah Valley in Virginia and J. I. Case of Racine, Wisconsin, designed and manufactured new farming **implements** (**im** pluh muhnts). In 1847, McCormick built his Chicago factory to manufacture his mechanical horse-drawn **reaper**, which made harvesting much simpler. And in 1892, J. I. Case manufactured the first gasoline-powered tractor. Both companies developed other farming equipment as well.

Inventions like this **threshing** tractor from Ogema, made farming much easier.

Mechanized equipment made it possible for farmers to plant more acres of land. The landscape in much of the state began to look very different as more acres of land were cultivated. Prairies in southern and western Wisconsin became fields of wheat. By 1860, Wisconsin ranked second only to Illinois as the nation's top wheat-producing state.

Settlers came to farm, and they found wheat easy to grow. But the wheat **boom** was short-lived. Wheat wore out the soil after just a few seasons. That's because wheat used up many of the **nutrients** (**noo** tree uhnts)

---

mechanized: Worked by machines **implements:** Tools or machinery **reaper:** A machine for cutting and harvesting grain
boom: A sudden growth **nutrients:** Proteins, minerals, and vitamins that help people, plants, and animals stay healthy
threshing: Separating grain from its husk

in the soil. Farmland that was once fertile stopped producing as much as it had in the past. Many wheat farmers decided to try their luck on the much larger **grassland** prairies on the Great Plains west of Wisconsin.

Wheat farmers who remained in Wisconsin found that producing wheat became more and more difficult. When more wheat was grown on the Great Plains, Wisconsin farmers earned less for their crops. Then from 1864 to 1866 **chinch bugs devoured** most of the state's wheat crop! One farmer in River Falls kept growing wheat. In 1886 he complained, "Where 3 years ago I had over 3,000 bushels . . . this year I had 843." A few years later another Chippewa Valley farmer sold no wheat at all.

But wheat was never the only crop grown in Wisconsin. The farmers who remained and the new farmers who arrived and planned to stay in the state wanted to keep their soil fertile and their fields full of healthy crops. They had to experiment to see which crops would do best on their land.

chinch bug

Beginning in the late 1800s, state government leaders and agriculture professors from the University of Wisconsin worked with farmers to find the best solutions to keep their farmland productive. The agriculture **experts** encouraged farmers to **diversify** (duh **vur** suh fı) their crops and livestock. These experts believed that by growing crops and raising animals that worked well with the land, they would be more profitable.

grassland: A large, open area of grass with few trees **chinch bugs:** Small black-and-white insects with red legs
devoured: Ate something quickly and completely **experts:** People who know a lot about a subject
diversify: To grow different kinds of crops or raise a variety of animals

Feeding the chickens

Edgar Krueger with twin calves on his family's farm near Watertown, 1906

What crops did Wisconsin farmers grow? In southern Wisconsin, some farmers grew tobacco. Others grew hops, which were used to brew beer. Farmers in the Central Plain began cranberry farming and potato farming. They grew oats, hay, and corn to feed their animals—including sheep, cows, and chickens. All of these new crops worked well with the region they were grown in. Because of the wise choices farmers made, Wisconsin became both America's dairyland and a state with a wide variety of crops other than wheat.

Becoming the Dairy State

People from Wisconsin were not always known as cheeseheads! The black-and-white Holstein dairy cow began to be an important part of the state's agriculture only after wheat failed. Dairy cows demand more attention than wheat. Once planted, wheat grows by itself until harvest time. Milking cows takes place twice a day, *every* day. But that wasn't the only reason that dairying arrived late in Wisconsin.

Pioneer farmers produced only enough milk and vegetables to feed their own families. Farmers needed to make many changes in order to produce good milk to sell year-round. Farmers needed more cows, and they needed to feed and house their cattle over the long winters. They also needed to build large, solid barns to keep their herds of cattle warm and safe all winter long.

But how could farmers store plenty of feed and keep it from spoiling? The answer was **silos**. Today silos appear so often that they seem to be almost a natural part of the rural landscape. But silos were a new solution in the 1880s and 1890s. It took several years of experimenting to find the right shape for the silo. Farmers found that the round cylinder-shaped silo helped prevent the **silage** (sɪ ludj) from spoiling.

Dairy farm families were used to milking cows and making butter for themselves. Selling larger amounts of dairy products to others was another matter. These dairy products had to **maintain** a quality that was high *and* **consistent**. Selling dairy products meant making changes in dairying.

A silo on a Wisconsin farm. Why would a man be on top of the silo?

silos: Round towers used to store food for farm animals   **silage:** Grass or hay stored and used to feed farm animals
maintain: To keep up   **consistent:** The same each time

Farmers need to grow a lot of feed if they have a dairy herd. It takes about 2 acres of hay to feed a single cow through a winter. But only one acre of grain (corn, oats, or barley, for example) can feed 3 cows. These grains also keep their **quality** (**kwahl** uh tee) longer and provide the cows with more nutrition than hay.

A man and a little girl milking a cow with a pail in 1924.

Luckily, many of the leading dairy farmers and cheese-makers in Wisconsin came from New York and from places in Europe, like Switzerland and Germany, where they had already learned dairy skills. They taught their neighbors in Wisconsin about special **breeds** of dairy cattle and about the complicated process of cheese-making.

Dairy producers built factories to **process** milk and cheese near dairy farms. Both dairy owners and farmers needed good roads to **guarantee** (ger uhn **tee**) that the milk would travel quickly and arrive unspoiled at the factory. And Wisconsin farmers were lucky! They often had to remove glacial rocks from their fields before plowing. They found that these rocks could be crushed to make some of the best gravel around. And this gravel, in turn, made Wisconsin's farm roads some of the finest in the country. Without those well-paved roads, it would have been impossible to deliver fresh milk quickly.

 quality: Good condition **breeds:** Different kinds of the same animal **process:** To prepare by a series of steps
guarantee: Promise something will definitely happen

Wisconsin farmers also wanted to improve the **dairy industry** by improving the quality of the milk they were producing. Farmers sold milk by weight. Some farmers cheated. They mixed water into their milk. Others skimmed the cream from the milk. Those farmers who cheated damaged the **reputation** of the whole dairy industry. Buyers wanted their milk to be consistent and high quality.

Professor Stephen Babcock at the University of Wisconsin went to work on this problem. He wanted to test the amount of butterfat in the milk. If the amount of butterfat was consistent, then the quality of the milk would be consistent. He wanted the test to be simple enough that it could be used by every dairy. In 1890, he successfully created what became known as the Babcock Test. Now that butterfat could be measured, the standards for good milk could be fixed. Milk buyers could now trust the quality of the milk they were buying. High-quality milk was either bottled or turned into cheese. Stephen Babcock's invention improved the dairy industry in Wisconsin and throughout the United States.

Dairying reshaped the landscape of Wisconsin even more than wheat had done. Cattle and feed crops—corn, oats, hay, and other grains—replaced

It was common to have milk delivered to your door in 1950.

The butterfat tester designed by Stephen Babcock showed how much fat was in cow's milk.

wheat fields. Farmers learned about new developments in farming by working with **county extension agents** and by reading magazines like *Hoard's Dairyman.*

Farmers learned their lessons well. For example, there were about 1,800 dairy cows in Wood County in 1880, and 30 years later there were 18,000! By 1900, feed crops covered 90 percent of Wisconsin's cropland. Wisconsin had become America's dairyland.

WILLIAM HOARD AND *HOARD'S DAIRYMAN*

William Hoard was one of those people who moved from New York to Wisconsin in the mid-1800s. He had already seen dairy farms replace wheat farming in New York. He wanted to help Wisconsin farmers make that big **transition** (tran **zish** uhn). William Hoard wrote newspaper articles about good dairy-farming practices. In 1885, he began publishing *Hoard's Dairyman.* This magazine had plenty of information to help dairy farmers. He also started his own farm so that he could practice the ideas he was sharing with others. Like the dairy industry Hoard did so much to help, *Hoard's Dairyman* is still going strong—it's over 120 years old! You can visit the Hoard home in Fort Atkinson, which is now the Hoard Museum and National Dairy Shrine.

Courtesy of Hoard Magazine

county extension agents: People who learn about the land and help people like farmers by sharing what they know
transition: Change from one thing to another

Changes in Dairyland

The number of dairy farms continued to grow. Dairy farmers were getting top prices for the milk they produced when the Great Depression hit in the early 1930s. Milk prices tumbled. The situation was even worse for small farmers. Larger dairies soon forced smaller farmers out of business. The number of dairy farms began to drop. The total amount of land that was farmed dropped as well.

But here's where things get confusing. The amount of milk that farms produced actually kept growing even while the number of farms fell. How did that happen? Technology played a large role. Mechanized equipment made it possible to milk a lot of cows at one time. Farms got bigger, but there were fewer farms and fewer farmers. These farms were able to grow more food on less land. And not just in Wisconsin. In 1996, huge factory farms in California helped

At the 1900 State Fair in West Allis, cows are lined up to be judged.

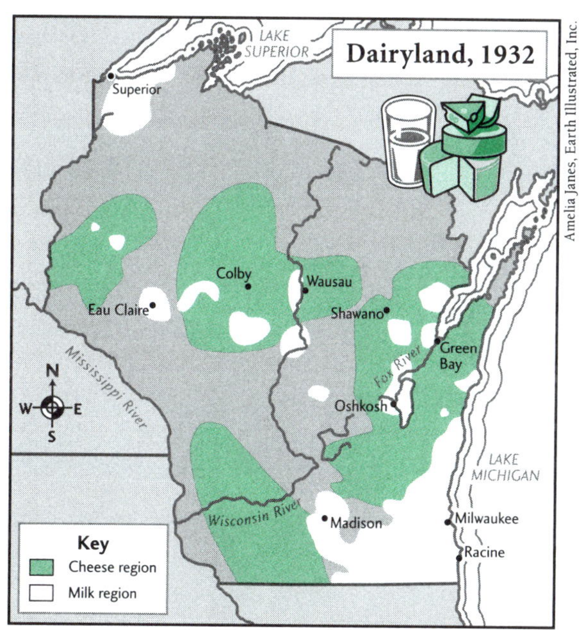

Year	Number of Farms	Milk Production (billions of pounds)
1930	170,000	11
1950	145,000	15
1970	65,000	18
1990	32,000	24
2008	15,000	24.5

Source: USDA/NASS Milk Production

make it the nation's largest milk-producing state. But Wisconsin remains the leader in cheese.

Although the number of dairy farms was still decreasing in the early 2000s, Wisconsin's dairy industry had already begun to grow in a new direction: **organic** (or **gan** ik) dairying. Today Wisconsin is one of the 2 top organic dairy states in the country and home to the largest organic milk **co-op** (**koh** op). Even though organic dairying is just a tiny part of the overall dairy industry in Wisconsin, it is growing instead of shrinking. And that's a very positive sign!

organic: Produced without artificial materials   **co-op:** Store or building in which members own shares of the business. Short for cooperative (koh **op** ur uh tiv)

Many Farms, Many Crops, Many Different People

Dairy farming and crops planted to feed animals suited the soil and climate of much, but not all, of the state. Most of the central and northern counties have a cooler climate and sandy soil. Cooler climate and sandy soil do not work well for dairy farms. These counties stretch from Door in the east across the central plains of Portage, Waupaca, Juneau, Adams, and their neighbors, plus Chippewa, Barron, and Dunn in the northwest. Fields there have been excellent for growing many kinds of fruit and vegetables. Non-Indian farming families arrived in all of these counties later than the farmers who settled in counties in the southern part of the state or next to the Mississippi River, Lake Michigan, or Lake Superior.

The Hemstead farm, located in Vernon County, is one of over 500 Wisconsin family farms of Organic Valley, the nation's largest organic co-op.

By the 1900s, Wisconsin's farmers were already the leading growers of potatoes, peas, beans, cabbage, cranberries, and cherries. These fruits and vegetables remind us that our state has a wide range of land types. Crops need to be selected to suit all kinds of land. That's why Wisconsin's many different crops continue to work best. Growing many kinds of crops is known as crop diversity.

Farm families worked together to test new methods of farming to protect their land. Eroding soil was a big problem in the state at one time. In the 1930s, **contour farming** (**kahn** tor) helped land became more productive. Traditionally,

contour farming: Farming on slopes in a way that keeps water from washing away the land

Contour farming near La Crosse in 1950. Can you see how the rows follow the shape of the hills?

A Mexican family stands outside their home in Plymouth in 1948. The house belonged to the cannery they worked for.

farmers planted crops in straight rows, no matter how the land was formed. In contour farming, the rows follow the contours or shapes of the land. Contour farming helps to prevent soil from washing away.

Remember that season after season of planting wheat had worn out the soil. Other crops that were planted in the same field year after year also wore out the soil. Just as Indian nations had done, farmers began to rotate their crops. They planted a different crop in the field from season to season. For example, a field planted with corn one year might be planted with alfalfa the next year. Just as the Oneota discovered thousands of years ago when they moved their gardens from one location to another, the soil needs change to make crops **thrive** . Rotating crops helps the soil remain fertile.

Selling What You Grow

This map shows the crops grown **for market** in our state. You can see when each of those crops was introduced in Wisconsin.

In 1887, the first **cannery** opened in Manitowoc (**man** uh tuh wawk). That's when a

    thrive: Do well   **for market:** Grown to sell to others   **cannery:** A factory that cans food

local pea grower built a factory to process his peas. By the early 1900s, canneries provided new jobs for many local people. Seasonal workers, known as **migrants** (**mı** gruhnts) also decided to work in canneries. This was especially common in the eastern and central counties of the state. Some migrant families settled permanently in Wisconsin. **Agricultural** diversity encouraged the growing diversity of Wisconsin people as groups of newcomers moved into farming communities.

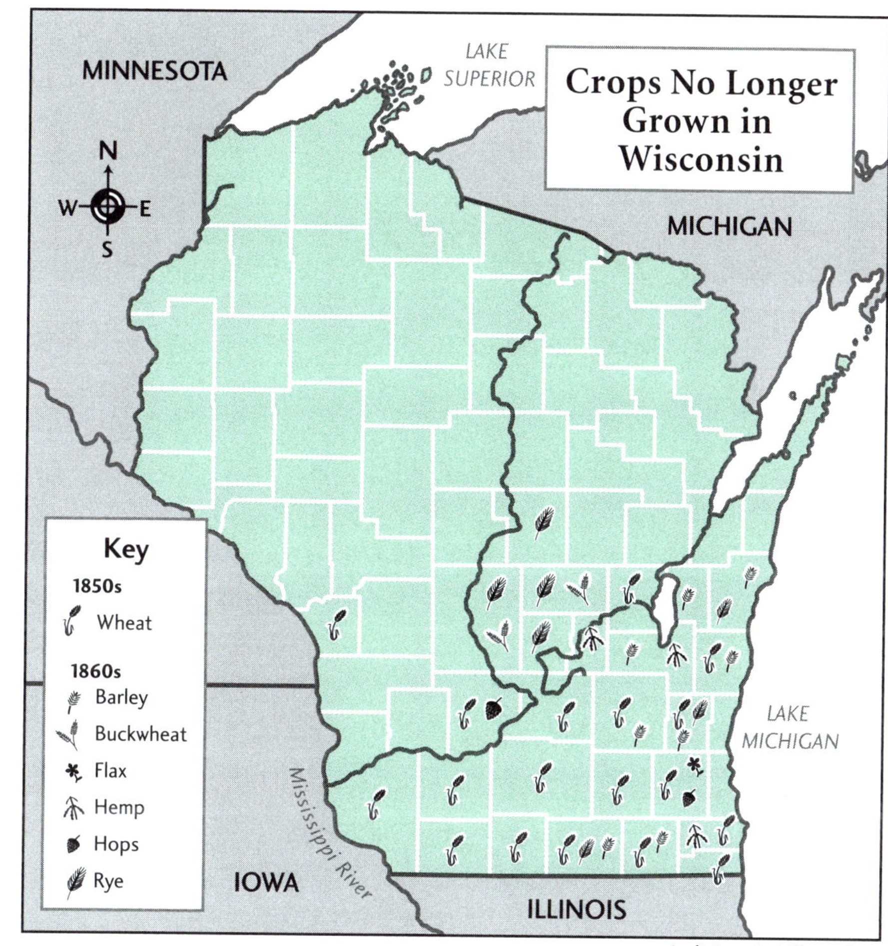

Amelia Janes, Earth Illustrated, Inc.

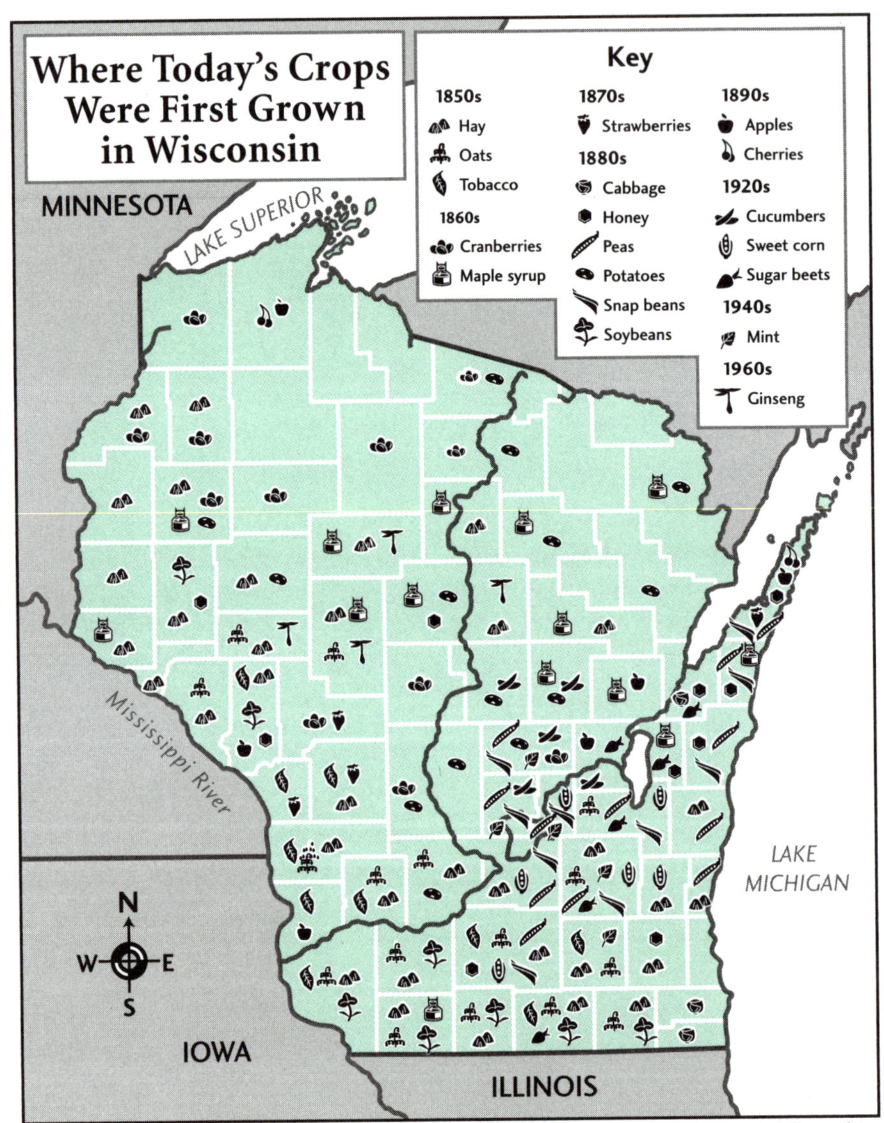

Amelia Janes, Earth Illustrated, Inc.

CRANBERRIES: WISCONSIN'S SPECIAL CROP

One special Wisconsin crop is the cranberry. It has been harvested in different ways over time. Indian people gathered cranberries from the marshlands of central Wisconsin for centuries. Cranberries became big business beginning in the late 1800s—especially in Jackson, Juneau, Monroe, and Wood counties. That's when the state worked to become the largest cranberry producer in the nation. Today, mechanized equipment makes harvesting cranberries easier and faster. Controlling marsh and river areas to flood cranberry marshes also has changed the natural environment of the area.

These pictures are from 1950 and 1997. You can also look at page 94 for a picture from 1913. How do you think cranberry harvesting has changed over the years?

As different people from different cultures and backgrounds moved into Wisconsin during the 1900s, other forms of agriculture developed in different areas around the state. People brought with them many ways of working the land. They introduced more crops for market. In the 1920s, farmers began raising sweet corn, sugar beets, and cucumbers for market, and in the 1940s, farmers first started raising and selling different varieties of mint.

A **combine** (**kahm** bɪn) harvesting corn

The Fromm brothers of Hamburg, Wisconsin, in Marathon County, for example, were the first farmers in Wisconsin to successfully cultivate **ginseng** (**jin** seng) in 1904. Farmers in Marathon County have been growing ginseng ever since. The ginseng root is prized in Chinese medicine and has grown more popular in other countries as well. Marathon County's cooler summers, hilly landscape, good soil,

Workers preparing the beds for ginseng plants to be grown in Wausau, 1938

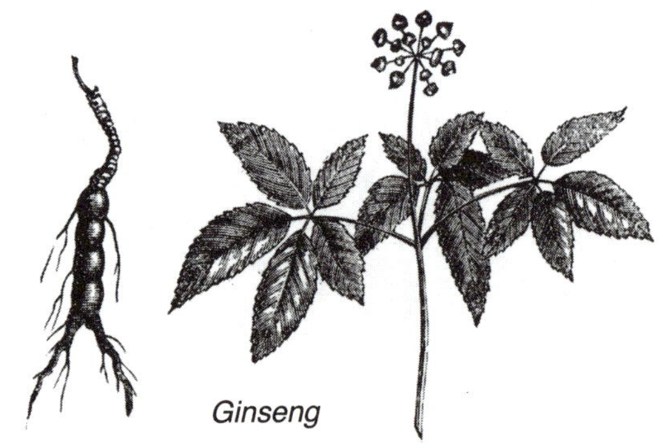
Ginseng

   combine: A farm machine used to harvest crops with long stalks, like corn and wheat   **ginseng:** An Asian plant grown for its root

and farm families who have been growing the crop for many generations help make Wisconsin ginseng the best in the world. Wisconsin farmers produce 95 percent of American ginseng. They ship most of it to Hong Kong in China. Since the 1960s, more people around the world recognized ginseng's **nutritional** (noo **trish** uh nuhl) benefits, so Wisconsin farmers cultivated more ginseng to meet the growing demand.

By the end of the first decade of the twenty-first century, Wisconsin's leading farm products start with dairy. We are still number 1 in the country for cheese, and number 2 for milk. Farmers market many kinds of **livestock** and **poultry** (**pohl** tree), including cattle, hogs, pigs, turkeys, chickens, mink, and honey bees. Farmers in Wisconsin grow more corn for silage, grain, cranberries, cabbage for kraut, and snap beans for processing than any other state. But farmers here also market honey, hay, oats, tart cherries, maple syrup, spearmint, peppermint, and many, many other kinds of crops. All have proved important to Wisconsin's economy.

Door County is known for its delicious cherries.

Eating and Buying Locally

In the later years of the 1900s, people around Wisconsin and the rest of the United States began worrying more about the health of children and adults. Too many people were sitting around too much of the time and eating too much snack food and making other unhealthy choices. Two ideas seemed to come together about the same time: eating better and healthier by growing and eating more food closer to where we live.

nutritional: Having to do with healthy eating **livestock:** Farm animals other than poultry
poultry: Birds raised on a farm

A Hmong family selling vegetables at the Dane County Farmers Market in Madison, 1997

Children arranging vegetables at a Milwaukee Farmer's Market in 1948

Local **farmers' markets** farmers' markets have played a major role in this **trend** toward taking better care of ourselves. Farmers' markets are not new. Since the mid-1800s, some cities have had areas where farmers sold their produce during growing season. But now that people are trying to support eating locally grown and produced food, families all over the state can find farmers' markets near them. Local farmers sell their produce around the Iron County Courthouse in Hurley during growing season just as they do around the state capitol in Madison. Many farmers' markets, like those in West Allis and Madison, only allow farmers at the market who raise what they sell.

    farmers' markets: Markets where produce and goods from farms are sold directly to customers instead of at the grocery store   **trend:** Pattern

Wisconsin Farmers' Markets Today
LAKE SUPERIOR
MICHIGAN
MINNESOTA
IOWA
ILLINOIS
LAKE MICHIGAN
Mississippi River
Wisconsin River
WISCONSIN
N W E S
Cornucopia
Eagle River
Phillips
Ladysmith
Catawba
Crivitz
Merrill
Antigo
New Richmond
Marinette
Sister Bay
Fish Creek
Hudson
Wausau
Jacksonport
Menomonie
Eau Claire
Shawano
Sturgeon Bay
Tigerton
Marshfield
Green Bay
Seymour
Pittsville
Oneida
De Pere
Waupaca
Wrightstown
Wisconsin Rapids
Dale
Appleton
Mishicot
Black River Falls
Kaukauna
Menasha
Neenah
Brillion
Two Rivers
Stockbridge
Chilton
Manitowoc
Oshkosh
New Holstein
Kiel
Holmen
Tomah
Berlin
Elkhart Lake
Onalaska
Princeton
Ripon
Sheboygan
La Crosse
Mauston
Green Lake
Fond du Lac
Plymouth
Waupun
Mayville
West Bend
Horican
Port Washington
Gays Mills
Grafton
Hartford
Cedarburg
De Forest
Germantown
Thiensville
Menomonee Falls
Wauwatosa
Brown Deer
Oconomowoc
Fox Point
Madison
Delafield
Dousman
Milwaukee
Rome
Bay View
Paoli
Waukesha
Cudahy
Fort Atkinson
New Berlin
West Allis
Belleville
Whitewater
Greendale
Brookfield
Hales Corners
Platteville
East Troy
Racine
Janesville
Burlington
Monroe
Lake Geneva
Kenosha

For many years, some families in communities have chosen to grow vegetables in their own home gardens. As more people choose to eat locally, more families are making home gardens. Others who live in apartments or have no space to make home gardens often participate in **community gardens** . Many communities in Wisconsin have community gardens. People who have immigrated to Wisconsin often plant vegetables in community gardens that are important to their own food traditions.

Another way that Wisconsin families have supported local farmers is by becoming a partner in a farm through a program known as Community Supported Agriculture (CSA). CSAs began in Germany, Switzerland, and Japan in the 1960s, but did not get started in Wisconsin until the late 1980s.

When people join CSAs, they and others become members of a particular farm. They **invest** their money in a "share" of whatever the farm produces during a growing season. Then, each week they receive a box of fresh produce. Some farms allow members to help pay for the produce by helping with the actual harvesting each week. Families who join CSAs feel that they are connecting to the farm families, their land, and their harvests. And they enjoy getting something different every week.

Growing Soil, Growing Vegetables, Growing Healthy

Farmers' markets throughout the state have helped people buy more locally grown fruits and vegetables. But that's not the only way people in cities get fresh produce. Milwaukee is one of the cities in the country where you can find **urban farmers** like Will Allen. This former professional basketball player is a leader in this movement in Wisconsin and across the country. His organization is known as Growing Power, and

  community gardens: Gardens shared by the community, where individuals each have a plot   **invest:** Spend money in hopes of gaining   **urban farmers:** People who grow crops in the city

Vegetables and fruits from Harmony Valley Farm in Viroqua are packed into boxes for CSA members to pick up.

A rooster from Revival Ranch Co-ops outside of Baraboo.

it is located in what he calls a "food desert"—a neighborhood with many poor people and no grocery store closer than 5 miles away.

Will wants *all* people to have **access** (**ak** ses) to fresh and healthy food year-round. That's especially important for poor people. Their health problems are in large part due to bad food, that is, food with little nutritional value. His solution? To start a farm in the city! Growing Power is an urban farm: greenhouses and farm animals that take up very little space and are right inside Milwaukee. Growing Power provides many healthy choices for people who did not have choices before Will Allen moved into their neighborhood.

access: The ability to use or buy

Will Allen was raised on a farm. Although his parents had other jobs, his father thought it was important that his children learned how to grow their own food. After his basketball career, Will missed working the land. He became an organic farmer on his farm just south of Milwaukee in Oak Creek. Will had been supplying fresh vegetables to farmers' markets and restaurants in the area. Then he bought a lot on Silver Spring Road on the north side of Milwaukee. It held deserted **greenhouses** that were once used to grow flowers. Will thought that he could begin a small store to sell vegetables from his farm. He hired local teenagers to help. When one group of students asked if Will could help them start a garden, Will's ideas began to change.

Growing Power's founder, Will Allen

   greenhouses: Structures used to grow plants, where temperature and light are controlled

At Growing Power, children learn about growing crops in an urban area.

"I had already been growing a lot of food in very little space out at my farm," he says, "but I wanted to bring that into the city." Will wanted to be able to grow food closer to the people who needed it. He also wanted to be able to teach people how to grow food themselves in cities where there was little space to do so. How did he accomplish this goal? First and most important, by growing good soil. Will says, "Soil is the number one thing. You can't grow food without it, [especially] if you're going to grow food like we do here." The better the soil, the more food you can grow in a limited space.

How do you grow good soil? **Vermiculture** (**vur** muh kuhl chur), using worms! You may already be familiar with composting—saving decaying food waste until it breaks down and can be used to enrich soil. Growing Power collects waste materials, like coffee grounds from local coffee shops or overripe fruits and vegetables from markets and restaurants. Worms are the most efficient workers in this process. Their castings (or "worm poop") become the rich fertilizer that makes the soil fertile. Growing Power grows millions of worms and makes many tons of soil each year.

vermiculture: Raising worms to make compost

The more worms, the better the soil for growing crops!

In addition to worms, Growing Power raises goats, chickens, turkeys, bees, and 2 varieties of fish—all of which contribute to a sustainable system. They also practice organic farming, not using human-made chemicals in their fertilizers. The greenhouses that once grew flowers now grow about 150 kinds of edible green plants—plants that are sold to the local community.

When asked if there's just one thing about urban farming that Will would want to tell students reading this book, he replied, "The one thing I try to get across to kids is how important it is to eat good food." Good food grows strong bodies, bodies that can exercise and grow strong and healthy. According to Will, it's really important "to get kids moving." He says, "Two hours of farm work is like 2 hours of working out for sports."

118

Growing strong and healthy bodies means eating lots of garden vegetables, as Will Allen points out. Growing your own vegetables makes eating them more fun, and gives you exercise as well. What's more, gardening makes you very aware of how you're using the land around you and what you can do to help that land be most productive.

Living with the Land

♦ ♦ ♦

Sometimes you have to make a difficult choice. Your best friend is having a birthday this coming weekend. You're invited to the party and to stay overnight. If you go, however, you'll miss joining your family and your favorite cousins on a trip to a nearby state park. Choosing one event will rule out the chances of doing the other—unless you are willing and able to adapt your plans. Perhaps you could go to the party, but leave before the sleepover so you don't miss the family trip. The choice you make is up to you.

The same is true with choices that we and our communities face about land use. Think back to the opening pages of the book where the example was whether to use land in a public park as a soccer field or a tennis court. Creating a soccer field would please soccer teams and disappoint tennis players. Building a new shopping center on open farmland near a **suburb** (**suhb** urb) would bring more jobs to an area. But the corn fields would no longer exist.

Choices force people to make decisions based on their **priorities** (prɪ **or** uh teez). When deciding how to design a park, people determine whether athletes play more soccer than tennis. When planning to build a shopping center, people sometimes try to construct the buildings and parking lots in an area without farms. That way, no fertile fields will be lost.

120   **suburb:** An area near a city where many people live in traditional homes   **priorities:** The things that matter most to a person

Milwaukee's skyline

As the number of people living in Wisconsin continues to grow, more people will be living in cities. These larger **urban** communities make it even more important for people to think about the consequences of the decisions we make about land use.

Think About It

Who has shaped ideas about the way land is used? How have these leaders helped us decide how to build the kind of communities that we want? What must we do to protect our natural environment? How can we keep natural resources safe from pollution? What buildings and other places of interest make communities special? What can we do to protect them?

A suburban neighborhood in Madison

urban: Having to do with a city

Looking Back

You've learned that people have been reshaping Wisconsin's landscape from the time they began living here thousands of years ago. At first, the changes were small and **gradual** . Then non-Indian people began to pioneer here, and lead mining, lumbering, and farming brought major changes to the land. Of course, not everyone who settled came to mine lead, cut timber, or farm. Many came to provide services. Road builders, doctors, lawyers, mill workers, storekeepers, cooks, railroad workers, teachers, and many others chose to make Wisconsin their home.

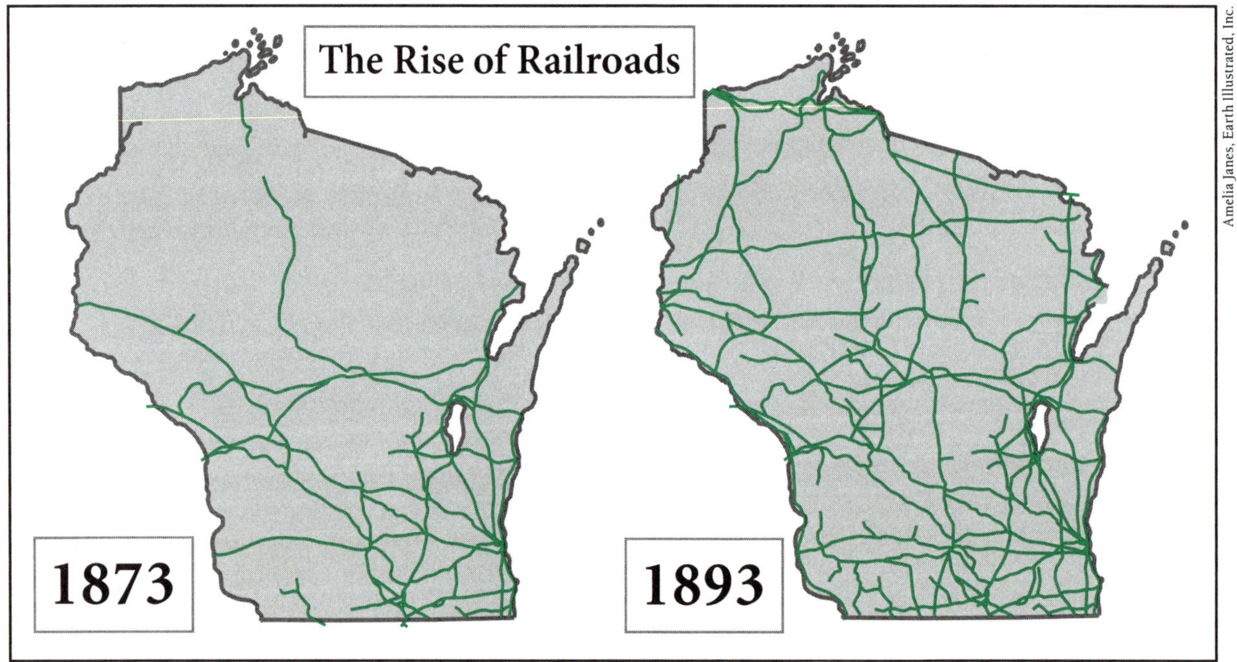

Why do you think railroads grew so much in the late 1800s?

  gradual: Happening a little at a time

As the number of people in the state grew, so did our towns and cities. The earliest Indian, European, and Euro-American settlements grew along waterways that people used for travel and shipping. Beginning in the mid-1800s, railroad construction in Wisconsin made it faster and easier to transport people and products from farms, forests, and industries. New villages, towns, and cities were built along railroad lines.

Then came the automobile. In 1918, Wisconsin became the first state to establish a numbering system for highways. The east-west highways were given even numbers, and the north-south highways received odd numbers. From then on, highways began to crisscross the state, linking people and places.

In 1956, the United States began to build an interstate highway system to reduce the time it takes to travel from states to other states and from major cities to other major cities. All of these roads increase the amount of traffic around cities. But many of these routes also cut through farmland or forests. As the number of cars, trucks, and buses has grown in urban areas, streets—and even

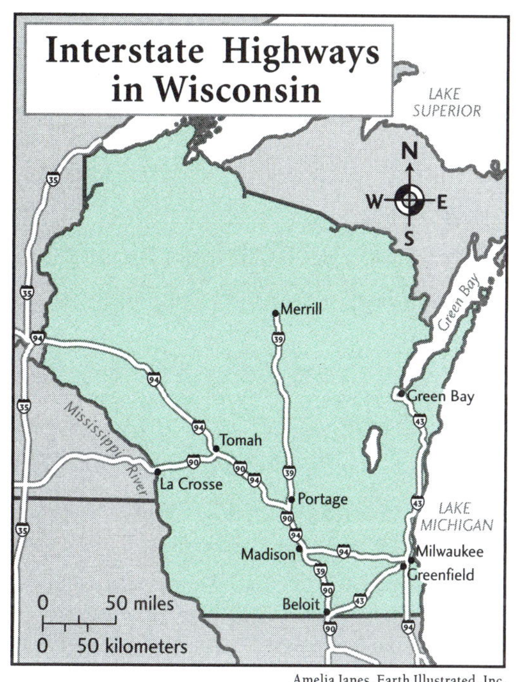

Amelia Janes, Earth Illustrated, Inc.

This photograph shows the opening of Interstate 94 in Waukesha County in 1958.

superhighways designed for speed—have become jammed during the most heavily traveled hours of the day.

Changes in transportation have made it easier for people to live farther from schools and workplaces. After World War II ended, people relied on the easy transportation of the automobile and began to build homes in the suburbs. Many workplaces expanded, and moved to the suburbs. Homes, shopping centers, and **strip malls** have grown up beyond older urban areas. Building these new homes, businesses, and roads also has created new problems.

All of this construction that forms the built environment has led to the disappearance of valuable farmland and natural habitats such as wetlands. Since 2000, some people have left the suburbs to live in cities once again. Of course, we need new neighborhoods for a growing population. But we need to learn how to grow and protect our natural resources. And we need to keep our urban centers places that we want to live in or visit.

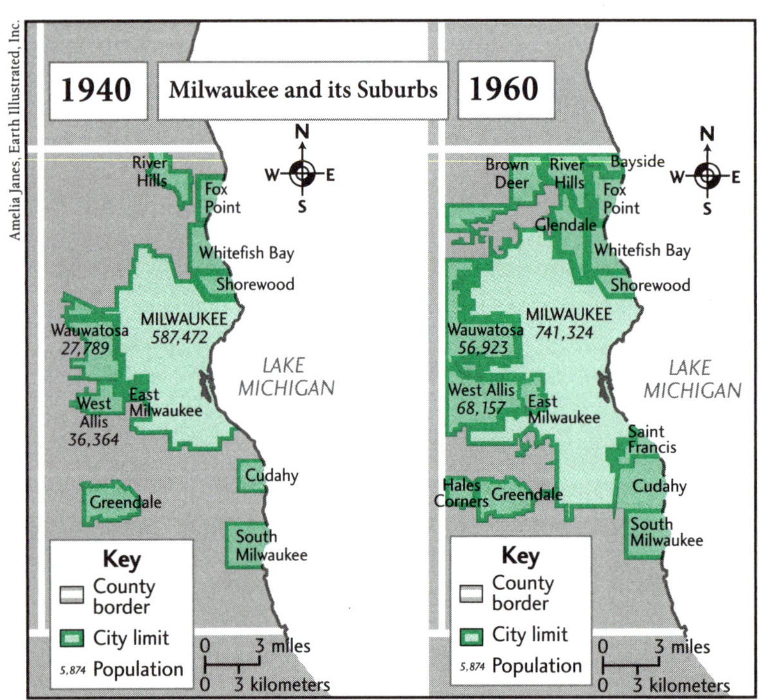

In what ways did Milwaukee County change between 1940 and 1960?

   strip malls: Shopping centers where the stores are lined up in a row with parking in front

Planning for growth can give people information to make good choices. Planning can help people of all **ethnic** , racial, and **income** groups create new neighborhoods *and* protect the things we already enjoy in our communities. That list of things that people value includes farmland and natural habitats. People also want to **preserve** important places in the built environment—downtown business buildings and places of worship, **historic houses** , and public buildings like courthouses or museums. And people definitely want bicycle paths, parks of all kinds, and other outdoor spaces for recreation.

*This historic home in Prairie du Chien, built in 1880, is known as Villa Louis (**vil** uh **loo** ee). It is a state historic site you can visit.*

Many people from Wisconsin have given us good ideas about learning to live *with* our land and to live *from* it. We'll look at the ideas from 3 of these lovers of the land: Aldo Leopold, Philip H. Lewis Jr., and Gaylord Nelson.

A Lover of the Land

Aldo Leopold grew up in eastern Iowa in the late 1800s. His home was on the banks of the Mississippi River. There he watched the passing riverboats and played in the **marshy** grasses along the river's edge. He also loved to tramp through the woods and to hunt.

But life along the river and in other parts of the countryside changed rapidly when more people and more industries settled nearby. As wild, unsettled places disappeared, so did the animals that lived in those habitats. Leopold wanted to do something to

ethnic: Having to do with a group of people sharing the same home country or culture   **income:** having to do with how much money one makes   **preserve:** To protect something so that it stays in its original state   **historic houses:** Homes that have special pasts and should be cared for   **marshy:** Grassy and with a lot of water

protect the environment that he loved. He realized that he wanted to work outdoors as a forester.

Aldo Leopold was an adult when he moved to Madison to teach at the University of Wisconsin. He had worked in different parts of the United States and had seen many areas where people had used land carelessly. At the university, Leopold taught **ecology** (ee **kol** uh jee). His students learned to think of the environment as a community of living things—including humans, but also including animals, trees and plants, and insects. He realized that if people were going to learn how to protect land, they first needed to respect it. But what could be done about land that had already been abused?

Leopold started an experiment. He bought a farm in Sauk County on the Wisconsin River. The farm was in terrible shape. The people who had owned the farm had cut down many of the trees, leaving a lot of open land. They also had tried to grow corn in the sandy riverbank soil. That soil wasn't meant to grow crops. Now it was worn out. The farm was in such bad shape that few wild birds ever rested there during their seasonal flights. Without forested

Aldo Leopold in front of the Shack.

Amelia Janes, Earth Illustrated, Inc.

   ecology: The study of the environment as a community of living things land, few animals found the farm a good place to make their homes.

The entire Leopold family worked to restore the land. They planted wildflowers, prairie grasses, and thousands of trees, especially red pines. Red pines originally had grown in the area where the farm was located. Pines were also Aldo Leopold's favorite tree.

The Leopolds cleaned up the riverbanks and turned a deserted chicken coop into a weekend cabin. They named their cabin "The Shack." After many years and much hard work, they began to see some welcome changes. Birds and other animals returned to the habitat Leopold and his family had restored.

Before he died in 1948, Aldo Leopold described life at the Shack in a book called *A Sand County Almanac.* "When we see land as a community to which we belong, we may begin to use it with love and respect," he wrote in the introduction. This was his idea for the **land ethic**, a way that humans could live as part of an **ecological** (ee kuh **loj** uh kuhl) community. He wrote about the beauty and usefulness of the land he and his family had restored and the joy they found by working with the land.

Aldo Leopold checks the health of a red pine.

Leopold's daughter Nina plants a young pine tree.

land ethic: A way that humans can interact with and care for the land **ecological:** How plants and animals relate to their surroundings

Many of Aldo Leopold's ideas may seem familiar to us now. That's because Leopold's teaching and writing in books like *A Sand County Almanac* have helped others to see the beauty that can return even to worn-out land. His words and actions have given us a good idea of what we need to do to rebuild our natural resources.

Designing for Tomorrow

For many years, Phil Lewis worked as a **landscape architect** (**ahr** kuh tekt) and **regional planner** in Madison. He learned from Leopold's ideas and added his own. For many years, he studied the Midwest by looking at where people have settled and how they have developed communities.

Lewis sees the land as a huge quilt with many patterns. He's found patterns of water, soil, plants, minerals, and people. But only *people* have the ability to make choices about how the land is used. He says that "if you're going to place patterns of people on the land, you should understand those different [land] patterns." Whether the pattern is simple or complicated, it's up to us to understand how the different parts work together.

Lewis believes that understanding land patterns should guide the decisions we make about

Phil Lewis shows students a model of an urban area.

landscape architect: A person who plans how plants and trees will look in an area **regional planner:** A person who thinks about the way that a large area of communities and natural resources should be arranged

land use. For example, if a **soil scientist** identifies good farmland, that land should remain planted in crops. That rich soil should not be developed into a shopping center or a neighborhood. Instead, new houses or shopping areas should be built on the **fringe** of a fertile area in order to preserve that farmland as a valuable resource. When people make decisions based on the kind of land in an area, we can have new neighborhoods and still protect the most fertile land for growing the food we need.

We want the best possible **quality of life** in our communities. We want our streets repaired and our parks and neighborhoods kept clean and safe. We want plenty of safe bicycle paths. We want buses or other forms of public transportation to take us where we need to go. We want our communities to make us glad that we live in them. And we want them to grow without taking over fertile farmland or harming wetlands or other natural resources.

People throughout history have added patterns of their own to the landscape. Certain places in and around our communities make us proud: effigy mounds, parks, and beautiful public buildings such as libraries, places of worship, or courthouses. These places in the built environment honor our **cultural** traditions. These places also create another kind of "quilt." It's also good to keep these cultural patterns in mind as we make decisions that affect our communities.

Lewis wants us to protect the best of both the natural and cultural patterns in our cities and towns and the surrounding countryside. He values forests *and* effigy mounds, farm fields *and* city parks, historic barns *and* courthouses. Lewis has discovered that most of the outstanding cultural *and*

Kids using the swings at playground in the public park at North Beach in Racine

The Mabel Tainter Memorial Theater in Menomonie, Wisconsin, was built in 1890.

natural patterns form "environmental **corridors** ," or "e-ways." He hopes that all kinds of citizens will work together to find solutions that make our cities, towns, and rural areas places where we enjoy living and visiting. Protecting and restoring these e-ways in rural and urban environments protects the places that are important to us.

Decisions that affect entire communities or counties aren't made by one individual. These decisions require people with many different points of view to work together. For instance, one person might know about the area's natural resources while another knows about **green building** . Working together, they can plan for the growth that benefits humans *and* the land.

We already know that we have to recycle cans, bottles, and newspapers. But Phil Lewis reminds us that we can also recycle *places*. In 1966, Wisconsin became the

   corridors: Paths   **green building:** Creating structures that save energy and are sustainable

first state to **convert** old and **abandoned** railroad beds into bicycle paths. Cyclists now enjoy peddling along the same routes once used by trains. This kind of land-use decision involves both imagination and cooperation. Going from train tracks to bicycle paths also tells us how people's needs for travel and recreation in this area have changed over the years.

This firehouse in Madison was built using environmentally-friendly products.

How can we keep what's good about our communities and improve things that are unhealthy or unwise? Lewis has studied the ways *all* communities are linked. He suggests that people from linked communities should work together as regional problem solvers. Lewis believes that we must be responsible for making both the natural *and* the built environment good places for all of those who live there.

Protecting Our Planet

Like Aldo Leopold and Phil Lewis, Gaylord Nelson helped people all over the country understand that individuals everywhere need to

A family enjoying an afternoon ride on Mariners Trail in Two Rivers.

convert: To make something into another thing   **abandoned:** Left behind

take responsibility for making good decisions about land use. Nelson grew up in Clear Lake, Wisconsin, and served as governor of Wisconsin before becoming a U.S. senator in 1962.

Gaylord Nelson

As a young boy, Gaylord loved playing and exploring outdoors. He was a young man during the Great Depression and worked for the federal government Works Progress Administration (WPA). Like the CCC you read about in Chapter 6, the WPA provided jobs for people who needed them. WPA jobs included building roads, bridges, parks, and schools. Gaylord worked in road construction. Playing outside as a boy and working in the outdoors as a young man may have helped convince him of the importance of taking care of our natural resources.

When Gaylord Nelson became governor of Wisconsin in 1959, he created the Department of Resource Development to make sure that growing communities had plenty of **green spaces** and natural recreation areas. He also created the Outdoor Recreation Action Program. This program allowed Wisconsin to buy land to preserve the state's outdoor recreational resources. Nelson earned the title of Wisconsin's **Conservation** Governor.

  green spaces: Areas without human-made features where people can enjoy nature   **conservation:** Keeping something from going away

Nelson's work on the environment ballooned when he was elected senator. He worked hard to set up a national Youth Conservation Corps. Thousands of young people would now be paid to plant trees across the country. Then he worked to pass the Wilderness Act, which allowed the federal government to buy and protect land across the country for outdoor recreation and other uses.

Many people remember Gaylord Nelson most for creating Earth Day on April 22, 1970. He wanted Earth Day to help people become more aware of the importance of our natural world. Nelson's idea for Earth Day worked. After the first celebration, both national and state governments passed stronger laws to protect our natural environment. Earth Day continues to be celebrated each year. It's a reminder of the responsibility we have to our environment, and to the future.

In his Earth Day 2000 speech, Nelson said, "We have finally come to understand that the wealth of the nation is its air, water, soil, forests, minerals, rivers, lakes . . . wildlife habitats, and **biodiversity** (bı oh duh **vur** suh tee). Take this resource away, and all that is left is a **wasteland** ."

Governor Nelson spent time teaching kids about the environment.

A crowd at the Wisconsin State Capitol supporting the first Earth Day in 1970.

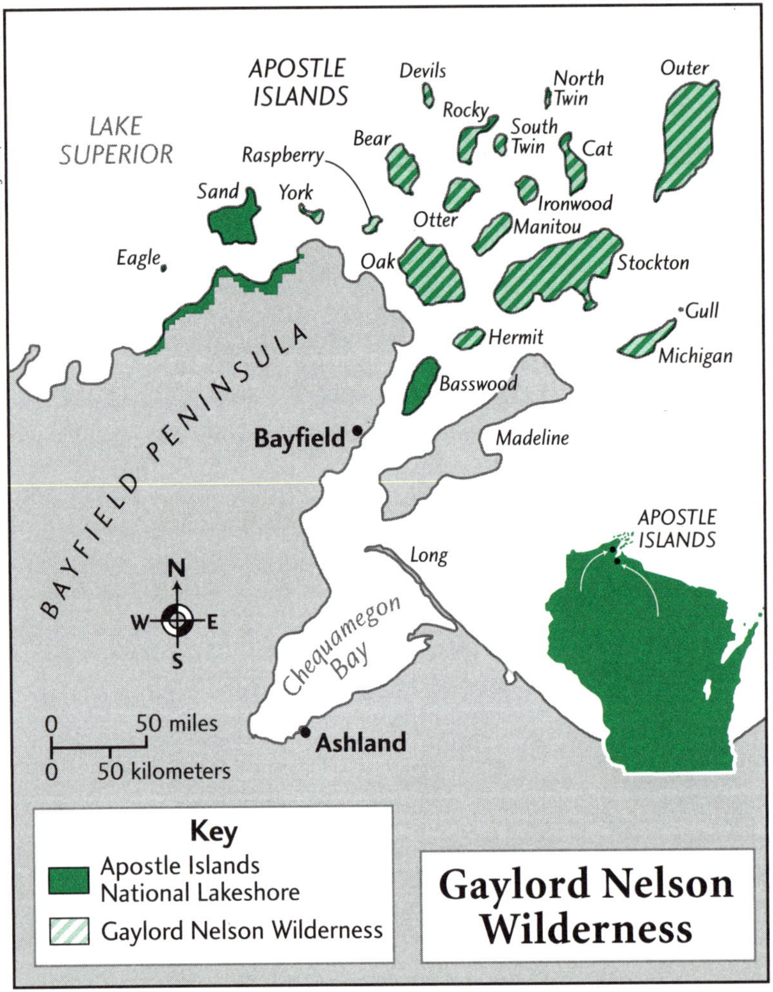

Amelia Janes, Earth Illustrated, Inc.

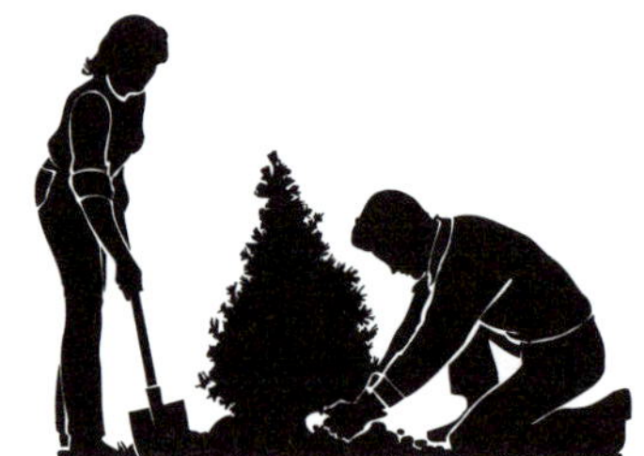

Aldo Leopold, Phil Lewis, and Gaylord Nelson all made choices that have made our state and nation better places to live. Since you are completing *Learning from the Land*, you are already learning to be problem solvers and decision makers. What is the best way for your community to grow? What special places in your community do you want to preserve? What land in and surrounding your community needs to be protected for farms, parks, forests, or animal habitats? What lessons have you learned from the land?

Glossary

Pronunciation Guide

a	cat (kat), plaid (plad), half (haf)	**oh**	open (**oh** puhn), sew (soh)
ah	father (**fah** THur), heart (hahrt)	**oi**	boil (boil), boy (boi)
air	carry (**kair** ee), bear (bair), where (whair)	**oo**	pool (pool), move (moov), shoe (shoo)
aw	all (awl), law (law), bought (bawt)	**or**	order (**or** dur), more (mor)
ay	say (say), break (brayk), vein (vayn)	**ou**	house (hous), now (nou)
e	bet (bet), says (sez), deaf (def)	**u**	good (gud), should (shud)
		uh	cup (kuhp), flood (fluhd), button (**buht** uhn)
ee	bee (bee), team (teem), fear (feer)	**ur**	burn (burn), pearl (purl), bird (burd)
i	bit (bit), women (**wim** uhn), build (bild)	**yoo**	use (yooz), few (fyoo), view (vyoo)
i	ice (Is), lie (lI), sky (skI)	**hw**	what (hwuht), when (hwen)
o	hot (hot), watch (wotch)	**th**	that (THat), breathe (breeTH)
		zh	measure (**mezh** ur), garage (guh **razh**)

abandoned Left behind

access (**ak** ses) The ability to use or buy

adapt To change because of a new situation

adaptations Acts of changing to a new situation

affected (uh **fek** ted) Influenced or changed

agricultural Having to do with farming

agriculture (**ag** ruh kul chur) Farming

ammunition (am yoo **nish** uhn) Material shot out of guns

ancestors (**an** ses turz) Family members from long ago

archaeologists (ahr kee **ol** uh jists) Scientists who learn how we lived in the past by studying the things people left in the places where they once lived

authority Power

bait Food used to attract something to be caught

bedrock The solid rock that lies under the soil and looser rock

biodiversity (bı oh duh **vur** suh tee) Many different kinds of plants and animals in one place

blazed Burned

boom A sudden growth

boundaries The lines that separate one area from another

breeds Different kinds of the same animal

built environment The human-made features that make up a landscape, such as houses, buildings, and roads

bureau (**byur** oh) Office

cannery A factory that cans food

cartographers (car **tog** gruhf furz) People who make maps

cede (**seed**) Give up

ceremonies (**ser** uh moh neez) Important acts done at special times and places

chinch bugs Small black-and-white insects with red legs

citizens (**sit** uh zuhns) Members of a particular community who have certain rights

claims Rights to ownership

combine (**kahm** bɪn) A farm machine used to harvest crops with long stalks, like corn and wheat

community gardens Gardens shared by the community, where individuals each have a plot

compost (**kahm** pohst) A mixture of dead leaves, grass, and food waste that is added to soil to make it richer

conduct To carry out; do

conflict Disagreement

consequences (**kahn** suh kwen sez) Effects

conservation Keeping something from going away

consistent The same each time

convert To make something into another thing

contour (**kahn** tor) **farming** Farming on slopes in a way that keeps water from washing away the land

convinced Swayed the opinion of

co-op (**koh** op) Store or building in which members own shares of the business. Short for cooperative

corridors Paths

councils Groups of people who discuss and make decisions

county extension agents People who learn about the land and help people like farmers by sharing what they know

county forests Forests owned and taken care of by state counties

crosscut saws Saws designed to cut into the grain of the wood

cultivate To plant, grow, and harvest

cultural Having to do with the way people live

culture The way of life, ideas, and traditions of a group of people

Cutover The vast stretch of land in northern Wisconsin that was heavily logged, leaving a cleared landscape

dairy industry Everything having to do with the business of dairy

dean Head

defeat Loss

demand Need

dependent Controlled by other people or things

deposits (di **poz** its) Natural layers of rock, sand, or minerals found in the ground

descendants (di **sen** duhnts) Someone's children and grandchildren and their children and grandchildren

desirable (di **zɪ** ruh buhl) Worth having

developer Someone who transforms land

devoured Ate something quickly and completely

disrupted (dis **ruhp** ted) Got in the way of; interrupted

diversify (duh **vur** suh fɪ) To grow different kinds of crops or raise a variety of animals

double A hit that earns the hitter 2 bases in baseball

dredged Dug or scooped out

ecological (ee kuh **loj** uh kuhl) How plants and animals relate to their surroundings

ecology (ee **kol** uh jee) The study of the environment as a community of living things

efficiently Working without wasting time

effigy (**ef** uh jee) **mounds** Indian mounds carved in the shape of an animal

elders Respected older leaders

entrepreneurs (ahn truh pruh **nurz**) People who start their own business from scratch

environment (en **vi** ruhn muhnt) The natural world of land, sea, soil, and air in which people, animals, and plants live

environmental education Teaching about how to care for the environment

era A period of time in history

established Put in place; started

ethnic Having to do with a group of people sharing the same home country or culture

Europeans (yur up **pee** uhns) People from the continent of Europe

evaporates Turns from liquid to gas

eventually At a time in the future

evidence Material that helps prove something really happened

exchange A system of giving one thing and receiving another

expanded Grew in number

experts People who know a lot about a subject

extinct No longer exist

farmers' markets Markets where produce and goods from farms are sold directly to customers instead of at the grocery store

federal government A type of government where a nation's states are united under and controlled by one government

fertile (**fur** tuhl) Good for growing crops

firestorm A fire of great size and heat that is fed by strong winds

fleeing Escaping from danger

forest management Using techniques to conserve and promote forests

forest preserves Forest land managed by the state

for market Grown to sell to others

fort A building built strong enough to survive attacks, sometimes surrounded by walls or tall fences

fringe Edge

fur trade The process of exchanging European goods for Indian goods, such as pelts or wild rice

galena (guh **lee** nuh) A shiny gray mineral used to make lead

game Wild animals that are hunted for sport and food

generation A group of descendants from a shared ancestor who are alive at same time

geographers (jee **og** ruh furz) Scientists who study the earth, including its people, resources, climate, and physical features

geological (jee uh **loj** uh kuhl) Having to do with the study of layers of rock that form the earth

geologists (jee **ol** uh jists) Scientists who study the layers of rock that form the earth

ginseng (**jin** seng) An Asian plant grown for its root

glacial drift The soil and rock that has been moved by ice

glaciated (**glay** shee ay tuhd) Once covered by large sheets of ice

glaciers (**glay** shurz) Sheets of ice that cover large areas of land

gorges (**gor** juhz) Large spaces between rocks

gradual Happening a little at a time

grassland A large, open area of grass with few trees

Great Depression The years following the 1929 stock market crash when many people were without jobs

green building Creating structures that save energy and are sustainable

greenhouses Structures used to grow plants, where temperature and light are controlled

green spaces Areas without human-made features where people can enjoy nature

groves Groups of trees growing or planted near one another

guarantee (ger uhn **tee**) Promise something will definitely happen

habitats (**hab** uh tats) Places and natural conditions where plants and animals live

hardwoods Broad-leafed trees that lose their leaves, such as birch, maple, and oak

hatters People who make hats

historic houses Homes that have special pasts and should be cared for

immigrants People who move to a new area from another country

implements (**im** pluh muhnts) Tools or machinery

income Having to do with how much money one makes

independent Free of the control of other people or things

industrial forests Forests owned and taken care of by industry

industry Everything having to do with one type of product

innovative (**in** uh vay tiv) Inventing new ways of doing things

interior (in **tir** ee ur) An area inside of another

invest Spend money in hopes of gaining

isthmus A narrow strip of land between two bodies of water

kettles Scooped-out areas that were filled with large blocks of ice

land ethic A way that humans can interact with and care for the land

landscape A large area of land that you can view from one place

landscape architect (**ahr** kuh tekt) A person who plans how plants and trees will look in an area

land stewardship Taking responsibility to care for the land so that resources will be available in the future

land use The way people have changed the land where they live by building on it, plowing it, making roads across it, and creating settlements or cities

lead shot Small pellets used in guns before bullets were invented

lease To rent for a period of time

ledger Book where money related to a business is written down

legal boundaries The lines created by the government that separate one property from another

legislators (**lej** uh slay turz) People who make laws

144

linear (**lin** ee ur) Long, like a pencil

livelihood (**lɪv** lee hud) Way of making enough money to support oneself

livestock Farm animals other than poultry

lodges Indian homes or dwellings

log drive An event each spring when logs were floated down the river in great numbers

lots Pieces of a township that individuals buy

lumber Boards sawed from logs at a sawmill

lumber industry The business of logging trees and turning them into boards and planks that can be sold to construct homes and other buildings

lumberjacks People who worked in the woods and loved in the lumber camps

lumbermen Forest and sawmill owners

maintain To keep up

mammals Warm-blooded animals with a backbone

managed Took charge of

manufacturers Companies that make something

marshy Grassy and with a lot of water

massacred (**mass** uh curd) Fiercely attacked and killed in large numbers

mastodons (**mast** uh dons) Large, hairy mammals, related to the elephant, that died out thousands of years ago

mature (muh **chur**) Full-grown

mechanized (**mek** uh nɪzd) Worked by machines

meridians (mer **rid** ee ans) Imaginary lines that run from north to south

migrants (**mɪ** gruhnts) Workers who move to where the work is

militia (muh **lish** uh) A volunteer army

minerals Solid substances like gold or copper, usually dug from the earth

missionary (**mish** uh ner ee) Someone who is sent by a church or religious group to teach the group's faith

modify (**mod** uh fɪ) To change a little

moraine (muh **rain**) Soil and rocks left by glaciers that form ridges and low hills

national forests Forests owned and taken care of by the United States

natural boundaries Features of nature that separate one area from another

natural environment The original features that make up a landscape, such as trees, rivers, and animals

natural resources Raw materials found in nature that may be used by people, like plants, water, animals, and minerals

146

nature preserves (pri **zurvz**) Areas where wild animals, fish, or trees and plants are protected

negotiate (nig **oh** shee ayt) Discuss something in order to come to an agreement

nomadic (noh **mad** ik) Moving from place to place to survive

nursery A place where trees and plants are grown from seedlings to be planted on state and private lands

nutrients (**noo** tree uhnts) Proteins, minerals, and vitamins that help people, plants, and animals stay healthy

nutritional (noo **trish** uh nuhl) Having to do with healthy eating

oak openings Prairies where oaks have been the only trees to survive past fires because of their thick bark

official Respected by an authority

ordinance (**or** duh nuhns) A law or command

organic (or **gan** ik) Produced without artificial materials

overlogging Logging all of the trees in one area so that none are left to reproduce

parallels Imaginary lines that run from east to west

peak The highest point

pelts Animals skins with the fur or hair still on them

physical features The appearance of the land, including its mountains, rivers, and plants

plantation A large farm

plat maps Maps of townships showing the boundaries of lots

plentiful Existing in large amounts

poultry (**pohl** tree) Birds raised on a farm

prairie A large area of flat or rolling grassland with few or no trees

preserve To protect something so that it stays in its original state

printers' type Metal letters used to print in early printing machines

priorities (prı **or** uh teez) The things that matter most to a person

prized Seen as valuable

process To prepare by a series of steps

processes Series of actions that produce a result

produce To make

proposed Suggested or offered an idea for discussion

protest Strong public disagreement

quality (**kwahl** uh tee) Good condition

quality of life How good the conditions are where people live

raid To take with force

raker teeth Teeth in a crosscut saw that get rid of excess sawdust as they cut through the wood, making cutting faster

reaper A machine for cutting and harvesting grain

recreation (rek ree **ay** shuhn) The sports or hobbies that people enjoy in their spare time

rectangular survey A system of exploring and measuring land using rectangular shapes to decide where boundaries should be drawn

reed A tall grass with a long, hollow stem that grows in or near water

reforestation (ree for uh **stay** shuhn) Planting trees to replace those that have been logged or destroyed by disease or fire

regional planner A person who thinks about the way that a large area of communities and natural resources should be arranged

regions (**ree** juns) Areas defined by common features, such as a similar landscape

related Part of the same family

removed Forced to move

reputation What others think of you

reunite (ree yoo **nit**) To meet again after being separated

road atlas A book of maps that show roads, boundaries between places, and important landmarks

rotated Switched from season to season

route A road or course you follow to get from one place to another

rural Having to do with farms or the country

sacred (**say** krid) Deserving of respect

sawmills Places where workers use machines to cut logs into lumber

school forests Forests owned by school districts to teach students about forest management

seedlings Young plants grown from a seed

selective cutting Cutting down mature trees so that younger trees may grow

shafts Tunnels going straight down into the ground

silage (**sı** ludj) Grass or hay stored and used to feed farm animals

silos Round towers used to store food for farm animals

skidways Riverbanks where logs could slide into the water

slash Branches, leaves, and twigs left after cutting a tree

smelter A place where metal is melted

sod The top layer of grass and soil

softwoods Cone-bearing evergreens such as pine, spruce, and hemlock

soil erosion (i **roh** zhuhn) The wearing away of soil by water or air

soil scientist A person who studies aspects of dirt

speculators (**spek** yuh lay turz) People who invest in something risky in order to make money

spiritual (**spir** uh choo uhl) Having to do with the soul

state forester Person hired by the state to care for its forest

stationary Not moving

stewards Caretakers

strategies (**strat** uh jeez) Plans

strip malls Shopping centers where the stores are lined up in a row with parking in front

suburb (**suhb** urb) An area near a city where many people live in traditional homes

sulfur An element used in gunpowder, matches, and fertilizer

surrender To give up

surveying (sur **vay** ing) Exploring and measuring land in order to make a map or plan

surveyors People who determine the geographic appearance or legal boundaries of a place

sustainable (suh **stayn** uh buhl) Using a resource so that it can be used today and in the future

sustainable yield forestry Harvesting fewer trees than the forest produces naturally

tapped Made a hole to draw out a liquid, such as sap from a tree

technology (tek **nol** oh jee) The use of science and engineering to do practical things

territory An area that a nation owns but does not call a state

threatened Put in danger

threshing Separating grain from its husk

thrive Do well

topography (tuh **pog** ruh fee) The physical features of the land that shape its landscape, such as mountains, valleys, plains, and rivers

townships Smaller parts of a town that have control over their land

tragic Sad and dramatic

transformed Changed in major ways

transition (tran **zish** uhn) Change from one thing to another

transportation Everything having to do with travel

treaties Agreements between nations

trench A long, deep, narrow hole

trend Pattern

unglaciated Not covered in the past by large sheets of ice

unjust Not fair

urban Having to do with a city

urban farmers People who grow crops in the city

urban forest The trees, plants, and animals found in a city

vermiculture (**vur** muh kuhl chur) Raising worms to make compost

wasteland A landscape without life

wetlands Areas covered with water for all or part of the year

World War II A war fought in Europe and Asia from 1939 to 1945

Index

This index points to pages where you can read about persons, places, and ideas. If you do not find the word you are looking for, try to think of another word that means about the same thing.

Sometimes the index will point to another word, like this: Boats. *See* Ships. When you see a page number in **bold** it means there is a picture or a map on the page.

A

Allen, Will, 114–119, **116, 118**
Archaeologists, 16, 20
Automobiles, 123–124

B

Babcock, Professor Stephen, 101
Battle of Wisconsin Heights, **51**, 52
Belmont, Wisconsin, **62**, 67–68

Black Hawk, Chief, 49–53, **49**, **51**
Black Hawk War, 44, 49–53, **51**
Blue Mounds, Wisconsin, 48, 51
Boundaries, legal and natural, 21, 56, 57
Brigham, Ebenezer, 47–48, 51
Bunyan, Paul, 78, **78**
Burial mounds, 20–21, **22**

C

Cartographers, 61, 64
Cheese-making, 100, **103**, 104
Chequamegon-Nicolet National Forest, 88, 91
Choices
    and building decisions, 120–121
    changes and choices, viii–1
    and community land use, 128–131

and landscape changes, 12–13, 25

Civilian Conservation Corps (CCC), 89–90, **90**

Climate, 12, 16, 105

Community gardens, 114

Community growth and planning, 58, 62, 125, 128–131

Community Supported Agriculture (CSA), 114–115

Compost, 24, 117

Corn, 10, 23, 50, 98, 100, 110

Cranberries, **94**, 98, 105, 109, **109**

Crop diversity, 97–98, 105, 106

Crop rotation, 24, 106

Cultural traditions, 129

"The Cutover," 84–85, **84**, 87

D

Dairy farming, 98–104

Dairy products, 99–101

Dane County, 47, 112

Decorah, Spoon, 47

Dodge, General Henry, 55, **55**

Doty, Governor James Duane, 55, 64, 65–67, 69

Driftless Area, **5**, 6–7, **6**, 8, 10, 45

E

Earth Day, 133

Ecology, 126

Effigy mounds, 20–22, **20**, **22**

Environment, built and natural, 2

"Environmental corridors," 130

Environmental education, 90

Europeans, 22, 27, 58

F

Factory farms, 103–104

Farmers' markets, 112, **113**

Farming
best farming areas, **95**
contour farming, 105–106, **106**
Crops No Longer Grown in Wisconsin, **107**
and Cutover land, 84–85, **84**
by Indians, 22–25, **24**, 31, 94
fertile soil, 8, 93–95
innovative farming practices, 23
and mechanized equipment, 96, 103
weather and, 92–93

Where Crops Were First Grown in Wisconsin, **108**

Fires, 23, 80, 82–83, **83**

"Food desert," 115

Food gathering, 17, 23

Forests
    in 1840, **70**
    clear-cutting, 83–85
    Forests Today, **91**
    and land stewardship, 89–91
    management, 85–87
    preserves, 86
    products, 73, 87
    types of, 88
    urban forests, 91

Forts, 51, 65, **66**

Four Lakes area, **67**, 68–69

Fox-Wisconsin Waterway, **66**

Fur trade
    about, 27
    growth of, 32–33
    Indian dependence on Europeans, 33–34
    map of routes, **34**
    and natural resources, 35–37

G

Geographers, 7

Geologists, 4

Ginseng, 110–111, **110**

Glacial features, 4–6, **4**, **5**, **6**

Great Depression, 89, 103, 132

Great Lakes, **63**, 64

Green building, 130, **131**

Griffith, Edward Merriam, 86–87

Growing Power, 114–118

H

Highways, **14**, 123, **123**

Historic buildings, 125

Ho-Chunk people, 43, 46–48, **53**, 69, **94**

Hoard, William, 102

Hunting, 16–19, 23, 31–32, 35–37

I

Immigrants, 45, 84–85

Indians
    Archaic Indians, 17–19
    Black Hawk War, 44, 49–53, **51**
    ceding of Indian lands, 53, **53**
    effect of fur trade on families and villages, 35–37
    land treaties with U.S. government, 40–43
    migration of, **28**, 49–53
    Paleo-Indians, 16
    tribes of Wisconsin, 28, **28**

using forest resources, 72

Woodland Indians, 19, 20–22

Insects, 97, **97**

Inventions, twentieth century, 26

L

Land developers and planned communities, 67–69

Land ethic, 126

Land Ordinance law, 59

Land stewardship, 89–91

Land treaties

and ceding of Indian lands, 53, **53**

and Indian ideas about ownership, 19, 40–42, 48–49, 58

and misunderstandings, 40–43

and rules, 38–39

and fairness, 42–43

Land speculators, 62–63

Land stewardship, 89–91

Land use, viii, 29–32

Landscapes, viii, 2–3, 7–10, 12, 15

Lapham, Increase, 85–86, **85**

Leopold, Aldo, **126**, 127–128, **127**

Lewis, Phil, 128–131, **128**

Livestock, 97–98, 107

Log drive, 75

Logging

camps, 76–77, **76**, **77**

companies, 78–80, 88–89

demand for lumber, 65, 70–71, 78

environmental impacts of, 80–84

and land stewardship, 88–91

tools, **73**, 76–77, 79

winter logging season, 74–75, **75**

Lumber industry, 70

M

Madison, Wisconsin, 9, 67–69, **67**, **68**, 112, **121**

Marquette, Father Jacques, 23

Marshes, 109, 125

Menominee people, **31**, 32, **28**, **29**, **53**, 72, **86**

Menominee River, 56, 82

Mesquakie (Fox) people, 28, **28**, 44, **53**

Michigan Territory, 55, **55**

Military Ridge, 65

Military Road, 66, **67**, 69

Milk, 100, 101, **101**, 103–104, **104**

Milwaukee, Wisconsin, 9, **60**, 114–116, **121**, 124, **124**

Mining
   copper, 17, **18**
   lead, 45–48, **46**, **47**, **49**,
      65
Mississippi River, 6–7, **6**,
   49, 50–51, **51**, **56**, 125
Mother Earth, 86

N

National Forests, 88
Natural resources, 17,
   18, 29, 35–37, 40–43,
   127–128
Nelson, Gaylord,
   131–134, **132**, **133**
Nursery, tree nursery, 87,
   87
Nutrition, 100, 107

O

Ojibwe people, 28, **28**, 29,
   30, **35**, **39**, **41**, 52, **53**,
   72
Oneota people, 24, 106

Organic farming, 104–105
Oshkosh, Wisconsin, 80,
   81
Overlogging, 85–86

P

Paper companies, 88–89
"Paper towns," 67, 69
Peshtigo Fire, 82–83, **83**
Physical Regions of
   Wisconsin, 7–10, **7**
"The Pinery," 73
Plat maps, 61, **62**, **68**
Potato farming, 98, 105
Prairie du Chien,
   Wisconsin, 36, 39, 45,
   67, 125
Preservation, 125, 132

R

Railroads, **79**, **80**,
   122–123, **122**
Recreation, 92
Recycling, 130–131

Reforestation, 87
Regions, 3. See also
   *Physical Regions of
   Wisconsin*
Rivers, 7, 56, 63–64, **65**
Roads, 65–66, **66**, 72,
   100, **123**
Rock River, 49, 50, 51

S

A Sand County Almanac
   (Leopold), 127–128
Sauk people, 28, **28**, 44,
   49, **53**
Sawmills, 73, 74, **75**, **81**
Seasons, 18
Selective cutting, 86
Settlers
   conflicts with Indians,
      48–49
   and land laws, 58–59
   need for land, 44–45
   purchase of ceded
      Indian lands, 53, 59
"The Shack," **126**, 127

Soil
  and farming, 8, 9, 12,
    93–95, 105
  of Wisconsin, 11, **11**
Soil erosion, 22
Soil scientist, 129
Star Lake Tree Plantation,
  87, 88
Statehood, of Wisconsin,
  53
Suburbs, 120, 124, **124**
Surveying, 59–61
Sustainability, 71, 86, 89,
  118

T

Technology, 26, 79
Townships, 56, 60
Trade goods, 33–35, 37
Trading posts, 36, **36**, **37**
Traditions, 19, 41–42
Trapping, 35–37

Treaties. *See also Land
  Treaties*
  1825 treaty, 39, **40**, **42**,
    43
  Treaty of 1804, 44,
    46–47, 49
Trees for Tomorrow, 89

U

University of Wisconsin,
  84, 97, 101, 126
Urban communities, 121,
  128–131
Urban farmers, 114–115
U.S. government, 40–43,
  53, 61, 65, 72

W

Waterways
  as boundaries, 57
  for transportation,
    63–65, **64**, 73–74, **77**

Wetlands, 6, 8, 9, **9**
Wheat farming, 95–97
White pine, 72–74
Wild rice, 29, **30**
Wilderness Act, 133
Wisconsin River, 9, **51**,
  52, 65, **66**, 89
Wisconsin Territory,
  53, 55, **55**, 65, 95
Women, 33, 46, **46**
World War II, 89, 124

Acknowledgments

The first edition of Learning from the Land and the accompanying teacher's guide grew from a series of collaborations that began in the summer of 1995 with Terry Saarela, Megg Heath, and Sarah Bridges at the Bureau of Land Management, Milwaukee District. The BLM generously supported our efforts. Within the Wisconsin Historical Society, those on board with ideas and critiques included Bob Birmingham, Diane Holliday, State Archeologist John Broihahn, Geoff Gyrisco from Historic Preservation, and Matt Blessing from School Services.

We gathered information and ideas from many sources, written and oral. Genuine teamwork from those within and outside the Society took place throughout the drafting and editing process. Among those who helped with different aspects of the publication are the following: landscape architect Philip H. Lewis Jr.; Kathe Conn, director of the Aldo Leopold Center; Dave Grignon, historic preservation officer of the Menominee Indian Tribe; Mindy James of the Wisconsin Geological and Natural History Survey; Connie Bodeen, graduate student in urban planning; Jeanie Schuldes, educator at the Neville Public Musuem, Green Bay; Marilyn Penn, Royal Oaks Elementary School, Sun Prairie; J. P. Leary, American Indian Studies Program, Department of Public Instruction; David Spitzer, Lincoln Elementary School, Madison; Wendy Sterne, Department of Education, UW–Madison; and Office of School Services volunteer Bill Bessler. Teri Hedges and Linda Robinson generously made arrangements for forth and fifth graders in classrooms at Huegel School in Madison and Allen-Field School in Milwaukee to offer ideas for the first chapter and activities. We heeded students' comments, and the final version of Learning from the Land reflects their many excellent suggestions.

For the second edition, several people offered expert reviews of portions of the text: Genny Finnouchi and Tessa Jilot of the Wisconsin DNR; Michael Douglas, site director at Villa Louis; Anna Haines of the Center for Land Use Education; Jerry Kaufman, professor emeritus of urban and regional planning at the UW; Sue Paulson of the Forest Products Laboratory; and Jeremy Solin of the Leaf K–12 Forestry Education Program. For the current volume, Society Press editor Sara Phillips worked with the author to update original material and add new content; Andrew White copyedited the manuscript; editorial assistants Carly Wieman and Sarah Michelle Klentz, together with image research John Nondorf, developed the art program; and production editor Diane Drexler guided the project through design and production.